Effectiv
Verbal
Communication

Denis Hayes
Series Editor: Professor Trevor Kerry

Hodder & Stoughton

A MEMBER OF THE HODDER HEADLINE GROUP

Note on Series Editor

Professor Trevor Kerry is well known for his books on the practice of teaching. He was formerly a senior LEA Adviser in charge of in-service training, and more recently has been a consultant and lecturer on aspects of education management. He holds a Visiting Fellowship in the University of East Anglia, and is Assistant Dean of the College of Teachers. He sustains his contact with the classroom by teaching on a regular basis and is an Ofsted trained inspector.

Dedication

This book is dedicated to the memory of my father-in-law, Charles Edgar Fielding, who introduced me to public speaking in 1969 and set such a wonderful example of kind and gracious speech.

Orders: please contact Bookpoint Ltd, 39 Milton Park, Abingdon, Oxon OX14 4TD. Telephone: (44) 01235 400414, Fax: (44) 01235 400454. Lines are open from 9.00 – 6.00, Monday to Saturday, with a 24 hour message answering service. Email address: orders@bookpoint.co.uk

British Library Cataloguing in Publication Data
A catalogue record for this title is available from The British Library.

ISBN 0 340 72541 9

First published 1998
Impression number   10 9 8 7 6 5 4 3 2 1
Year   2004 2003 2002 2001 2000 1999 1998

Copyright © 1998 Denis Hayes

Typeset by Transet Limited, Coventry, [...]
Printed in Great Britain for Hodder & S[...]
Hodder Headline Plc, 338 Euston Road[...]
Reading, Berkshire

Contents

List of tables iv

Statement of principles v

Editorial: Skills for the future vi

Introduction xii

Chapter 1   **The Power of the Spoken Word** 1
Activities 1–5

Chapter 2   **Clarity of Speech** 18
Activities 6–16

Chapter 3   **Speaking and Listening** 44
Activities 17–24

Chapter 4   **Classroom Talk** 67
Activities 25–29

Chapter 5   **Teaching and Learning** 84
Activities 30–34

Chapter 6   **Motivation and Class Control** 114
Activities 35–40

Chapter 7   **Speaking to Adults** 138
Activities 41–45

References 151

Index 155

List of tables

1 Desirable qualities for voices

2 Sources of anxiety in speaking

3 Reasons for inadequate communication

4 Positive forms of body language

5 Behaviourist theory

6 Constructivist theory

7 Social constructivist theory and classroom practice

8 A satisfactory learning environment

9 Questions pupils ask

10 Communicative networks

11 A comparison of co-operation and collaboration

12 Demands made on teachers' communicative abilities

13 Considerations in lesson planning

14 Characteristics of an authoritarian teacher

15 Characteristics of an indecisive teacher

16 Characteristics of a decisive teacher

17 Interpreting a pupil's actions

18 Teachers' responses to interruptions

19 Unwise statements

Statement of principles

The books in this series are based on a particular philosophy of teaching, which was largely developed (but not fossilised) in the 1980s as a result of the Teacher Education Project in the Universities of Nottingham, Leicester and Exeter – of which the series editor was Co-ordinator. This philosophy has stood the test of time and, it is argued, better meets the needs of teachers as professionals than some more recent developments, such as some competence models, which tend to trivialise the art and science of teaching. The principles of this philosophy are as stated:

Practical teaching consists of skills

- Skills can be isolated and identified
- Skills can be broken down into component parts
- Skills can be studied and taught
- Skills can be learned
- Skills can be reflected upon and refined
- Skills can be evaluated and assessed.

Each book takes a particular teaching skill and uses the latest research and practice to illuminate it in ways of immediate interest to all teachers.

Editorial: Skills for the future

The pace of change in society is constantly accelerating. This change is reflected in the world of education. Indeed, Drucker sums it up like this:

> *Every few hundred years in Western history there occurs a sharp transformation … Within a few short decades, society re-arranges itself – its worldview; its basic values; its social and political structures; its arts, its key institutions. Fifty years later, there is a new world … We are currently living through such a transformation.*
> *(Drucker, P (1993) Post-Capitalist Society. New York: Harper Business, p1)*

> *What will be taught and learned; how it will be taught and learned; who will make use of schooling; and the position of the school in society – all of this will change greatly during ensuing decades. Indeed, no other institution faces changes as radical as those that will transform the school.*
>
> *(Drucker, op. cit. p209)*

Yet it could be argued that even these changes have been modest in scope and pace compared with the changes that are likely to occur in the early years of the twenty-first century. Already the portents are visible of events which may affect radically *Schools for the Future*. These are just some of the changes of the recent past:

- the advent of the new learning technologies
- consumer choice and its implications for schools
- a redefinition of the nature of schools in the education process
- the changing place of Britain in the global economy and in the development of global markets
- concerns about environmental issues and the use of resources
- revaluation of the place of non-teaching staff in the education process
- the pressure to achieve 'more for the same' brought about by budgetary constraints and increased emphasis on targets and performance measures.

So how should schools be responding to these challenges, and what can be done to support them?

School responses

Schools are already exploring solutions for a changing world. Some of these approaches can be broadly categorised as follows:

Increasing the emphasis on learning

Traditionally, the world of education has concentrated on teaching, making the assumption that learning will follow inevitably. However, the emphasis of the late 1980s and the 1990s on assessing and recording standards of achievement has forced a re-thinking of this simplistic view. Students' learning rather than teachers' teaching is increasingly seen to be at the crux of the education process: the emphasis has moved from inputs to outcomes.

Re-aligning teachers to be 'directors of learning'

The increasing emphasis on the process of learning has caused many schools, and teachers themselves, to review the teaching function. Teachers often now conceptualise their roles more in terms of 'directors of learning' than as purveyors of teaching. The change is a subtle one which does not deny the traditional 'art and science' of teaching; but it concentrates more on the use of those skills to bring about learning in the student.

Assessing the implications of the new technologies

Among the most powerful resources which teachers, as directors of learning, have at their disposal is the developing technology bound up in Information Technology. This opens up entirely new avenues of communication, making access to data simple, self-study a powerful tool, and availability of information international.

Extending teachers' roles to be managers of the learning environment in its widest sense

Old-fashioned concepts of 'one teacher, one class' for primary schools, or of 'one subject specialist, one class' in the secondary sector are, in the scenario we have painted, as redundant in the twenty-first century as Victorian pupil-monitors are today. The teachers of the future may exercise less of a role in class control or in the traditional skills of exposition: they may well be the programme-makers and resource creators of the future. They will not 'do the teaching', they will manage (in every sense) the intellectual environment that students will inhabit.

Reappraising patterns of learning

One of the implications of the picture painted here is that not only will teachers' roles and patterns of working change, but so will those of the learners. With more and more computers home-based, even portable, not all learning will need to take place in schools as they are currently modelled. The purposes of school buildings and their patterns of use will become subject to reappraisal.

What must we do?

Education stands at a cross-roads. One of the ways in which some educationists are dealing with this is to establish projects, such as the *Schools for the Future* project with which I have been involved at the University of Lincolnshire and Humberside. The project is primarily intended to support developments and changes for this twenty-first century world. It is attempting to do this in a number of ways, as shown below.

Through an analysis of change as it affects education

The project will be alert for, and seek out, the global and national trends in education which are likely to affect schools and learning in the immediate future.

Through research into innovative practice

In particular, the project will seek out innovative practice, large- or small-scale, in Britain and overseas. Whenever possible, we will try to explore at first hand not just the problems and their solutions, but the decision-making processes and creative approaches which have been used.

Through a specific research project on the use of school time and plant

The project team is already involved with a Funding Agency project in a group of schools in London. Here we are experimenting with one of the fundamental issues to face *Schools for the Future*: the structure of the school day and the school year. This is a collaborative venture located in three schools in which we shall be monitoring and evaluating not only the outcomes (in terms of new patterns of attendance and their effects), but also the kinds of radical thinking which are used to arrive at solutions.

Through an examination of the developing uses of new technologies in schools

One of the keys to future developments in education will, inevitably, be the uses to which new technologies are put. These are already developing as a powerful tool for communication, and to a lesser extent for learning. These parallel developments are set to continue; and the ways in which they are adopted into, and woven into the fabric of, educational provision in the future are potentially very challenging to traditional thinking about schools and their functions. The project will seek to explore both innovation in this field, and to speculate about alternative models of learning.

Through an examination of the decision-making processes and mind-sets needed to bring about dramatic change

This project is about dramatic, rather than marginal, change. In the project's studies of innovative practice we shall be as concerned with the thinking process leading to change as with the change itself. These are largely uncharted waters, and we shall be breaking new ground in exploring this issue – which may have implications for the selection and education of leaders for the future.

Through dissemination of best practice

A fundamental purpose of this project will be to pass on to the education world the lessons which we are able to learn. We shall do this through whatever channels are most appropriate: visits, courses, conferences, books, journal articles, in-service training events, the Internet and the media. Our main concern will not be to provide examples of practice which others may copy directly in their own situations, but to tease out the principles which others may apply to reach their own conclusions in their unique situations.

What are the broad philosophies behind the project?

Schools for the Future is based on the principles of reengineering. Michael Hammer defines reengineering as:

> *The fundamental rethinking and radical redesign of business processes to bring about dramatic improvements in performance"*
> *(Hammer, M and Champy, P (1997)* **The Reengineering Revolution** *Handbook. New York: Harper Business, p3).*

At the heart of the reengineering philosophy is the client/customer. Reengineering is about providing a better service in a changing environment; but it is more than tinkering with structures to achieve marginally more acceptable results. Reengineering uses the best insights from other management theories (team-work, total quality management, etc.), but is much more than the sum of these parts. It is a mind-set that uses creative thinking in a focused way to achieve quite different ways of working. It is anticipatory rather than reactive.

Reengineering and teaching skills

This series of books of teaching skills has developed out of my interest in reengineering as well as from my long-term involvement with the initial and in-service training of teachers. Part of the intention of the series is to identify those traditional teaching skills which will continue to be fundamental to the teacher in the twenty-first century, and to provide a means of support for those who wish to acquire or improve them. Thus class management is likely to remain a fundamental skill for teachers: but its nature will change to accommodate the new roles for teachers as directors of learning and as managers of para-professionals in the classroom. However, other skills, such as the exploitation of the new technologies, are of recent origin and will have to be assimilated by all teachers, including those who perhaps trained for a school system which operated rather differently in the recent past.

Education is changing rapidly; and the nature of the teacher's job is changing, too. Some people find change only negative and disturbing. This series treats change as a positive phenomenon: one which challenges and excites. Hopefully, these books do not lose sight of traditional wisdom nor of the continuing values of which the profession is rightly proud. But they do look forward in a spirit of progression and development to where schools are going rather than to where they have been.

Professor Trevor Kerry
Series Editor

Introduction

The main purpose of this book is to help you, and those you teach, become more effective communicators of the spoken word; that is, to be more communicatively competent (Hymes, 1972). To help you do so, the book is divided into seven chapters covering topics about the power of the spoken word, improving clarity of speech, speaking and listening, classroom talk, teaching, learning and talk, class control and speaking to adults. To support your thinking and skill development in these areas, each chapter includes quotations, examples and activities. The activities are numbered for convenience but do not have to be used in order. References are listed at the end of the book.

Effective Verbal Communication is written for teachers working in every key stage of the National Curriculum, though lecturers in further and higher education should also find many of the topics to be of interest to them. The case studies offer a range of examples across the age phases from new entrants to post-sixteen students. The final chapter is exclusively about addressing adults, including giving formal presentations to larger audiences.

Social context is also an important factor in understanding the conventions of talk and appropriate behaviour during verbal interaction. Throughout *Effective Verbal Communication* we shall be examining in detail the impact of differing circumstances upon the relationship between speakers and their audiences.

For simplicity, learners will be referred to in *Effective Verbal Communication* as 'pupils' and those responsible for organising learning as 'teachers'. The learning environment will, unless otherwise stated, be called 'the classroom'. The term 'audience' will include any group of listeners. A 'verbal interaction' will describe occasions when two or more people are engaged in speaking and listening.

Talking words

What do you hear as you read this sentence?

> People hear but never listen; and listen but never understand; and understand but never believe; and believe but disregard. It would be better if they had never heard.

Try reading it again. Does it convey a different meaning this time? Has anything changed? Perhaps you read it incorrectly the first time or maybe you read it casually because it had little significance or perhaps, because it was the opening sentence of this book, you assumed that it was important, so gave it close attention. Whatever the case, it is likely that a second reading will provide different insights as you spend a little longer deliberating about its meaning.

If your motivation is sufficiently strong, you might be wondering what the writer is trying to say to you and whether your interpretation accurately describes what the writer was trying to convey. If the writer were standing before you, it would be possible to clarify things by entering into a dialogue based on your questions and the writer's answers. After a brief exchange, you would probably find yourself saying something like:

- 'Oh, yes; that's what I thought you meant...' or
- 'Oh, I see what you mean now; only I thought you were trying to say that...'

The opportunity to talk to the writer would assist you in your understanding and might lead to new insights and a fresh perspective on the issues involved. On the other hand, it could result in even greater confusion, depending upon the quality of the verbal exchange and the sense you made of his responses.

Words that have purpose

As you continue to read this page, you may already be wondering where this line of argument is leading. On the other hand you may be thinking that the ideas that are emerging are useful and you want to continue reading to find out what happens next. In writing the opening section, I have phrased my thoughts in a way which I hope will encourage you to look further into what I have to say. I have not been able to use techniques common to oral (spoken) speech, such as intonation, change of pace and gesticulation, so I have relied upon some open questions, careful explanation through word pictures, repetition of ideas and an intimate style. In this way I hope that I have compensated to a certain extent for the lack of visual cues and your inability to clarify the points with me that I have raised, and that you will want to continue exploring the ideas contained within the book.

Printed and uttered words

The printed word benefits from at least one major advantage over the spoken equivalent in that print can be continuously re-examined, thought about and analysed at leisure. One of the disadvantages of written language is that ideas, explanations and arguments have to be spelt out very clearly for the reader if the correct meaning is to be conveyed, as readers do not normally have access to the writer to clarify uncertainties or untangle ideas, and are left to make the best sense of it that they can unaided.

The spoken word, on the other hand, must be received and interpreted in the same instant. Unless the speaker pauses, the listener must rapidly synthesise a large amount of spoken material with little opportunity for evaluating its significance or questioning its authenticity or correctness. Professional commentators specialise in making instant summaries of complex statements, but the majority of us need thinking time to identify the main points and provide a suitable response to what is said. As Bruner (1966, Chapter 5) points out, listeners have to hold words and phrases together until they have opportunity to pull together what has been said. In listening, we can only interpret what is said as fast as words are provided by the speaker. The speaker, on the other hand, is organising ahead of what is said, drawing together the necessary thoughts and ideas, and translating them into speech. There is, therefore, always going to be a tiny interlude between what is uttered and what is received.

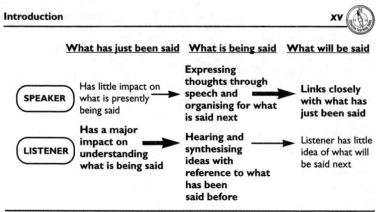

Figure 1 – *Speaking and listening*

Listeners also grasp what is being said by referring to previous statements or delaying their interpretation until the speaker has said other things that confirm the intended meaning or allow for it to be re-interpreted. Providing the relationship between the two persons is equitable and the circumstances are deemed appropriate, the listener may, under certain circumstances, interrupt the speaker to clarify points or offer supporting comment. However, if the speaker is perceived by the listener as superior or unapproachable, or there is an understanding between the speaker and listeners that interruptions are unacceptable, the likelihood of genuine dialogue is limited.

Effective verbal communication is also governed by social factors, personal values and background. We may be happily chatting away to a person on the train, unaware of the listener's status; if the person were to disclose his or her identity as (shall we say) a convict recently released from prison after a long jail sentence, our words might be more carefully chosen from then on! In some cultures, it is unacceptable for women to speak to men; in others, the reverse is true. Some cultures do not approve of maintaining eye contact with the person speaking, especially if they are of higher social status. Words can never be delivered neutrally; they are subject to interpretation which depend upon contextual factors as well as the delivery of the words through speech.

> Identities, values, mood and culturally ladened interpretative frameworks come into play as part of the ongoing co-construction of meaning. (Bowers and Flinders, 1990)

The spoken and written word differ in other important respects, not least that those in print offer the reader few clues about the tone, speed and emphasis that the writer intended. Good writers help the reader to 'hear' the words to convey the intended meaning more effectively. Speech, of course, does not include any visual punctuation, so the listener has to make best use of pauses and variations in the speaker's expression to gain a fuller understanding of the words and their meaning.

> A good writer is the visualiser who can make sound pictures clear; a good speaker is the visualiser who can reproduce the sound-pictures and make them clear to the listener. (Hulbert, 1932)

Understanding words

Even if I were sitting alongside you as you read this text, other factors would affect your ability to interpret my words. First, you would have to feel confident that your questions to me would be treated seriously and that you would not be made to feel silly for asking them or humiliated by the tone of my response. If such a thing were to happen, you would hesitate to enquire further; perhaps you would pretend that you had understood or change the course of the conversation to avoid further embarrassment.

Second, even if you felt that I was dealing appropriately with your concerns and treating you with respect, you would still have to know the right questions to ask. In part, the questions would depend upon the extent of your grasp of the issues involved, your past experience of dealing with the subject and your ability to handle the relevant vocabulary. If you had only a tenuous grasp of the issues, you might ask me to explain things in a different way. If you had limited experience of the subject, you would probably tell me what you already knew and assume that I would use this knowledge base as a foundation for elucidating matters further for you. If you had a poor vocabulary, you would stumble to convey your uncertainty to me and I might assume from your struggles that you understood less than was actually the case.

As the conversation unfolded, you would hopefully reach the stage where you had resolved your confusion and advanced your understanding of my ideas. In turn, I would understand better the nature of your uncertainty and have improved my own ability to explain things using different expressions, modified terminology and suitable analogies. Under ideal circumstances, we would both have benefited and gained from the verbal interaction, thereby enhancing our communicative effectiveness.

Introductory activity

Write down the name of celebrities who have a way with words that...

a) irritates you; b) enchants you; c) disgusts you; (d) captivates you.

1. Alongside each name write down two or three words which characterise their speaking.

2. Put the full list in order, starting with the most desirable one and ending with the least desirable.

3. Regardless of their manner, which of the people you have in mind are the best communicators? What makes them so?

Most of this book refers to classroom situations and the ability of teachers to enhance their own verbal communication skills. However, talking and listening is frequently used in classrooms in conjunction with written representations, and with other visual expressions such as paintings, drawings, models and so on. Effective communication relies not only on the words spoken, but upon the development of a creative and stimulating environment in which the verbal exchanges that take place are part of the fabric of learning.

Denis Hayes

Chapter 1

The power of the spoken word

The trick in every communication that has to work for you or help someone else, is to project the words away from yourself and on to the result you want.

(Howard, 1980)

Communicating with an audience

For the purposes of this book, an audience includes any group of people who are gathered for a specific purpose with a recognised leader. The audience may be a class of pupils, a lecture hall of students or a group of adults.

Howard's advice (above) reminds us that our words should be for the benefit of our listeners and not for our own satisfaction. Consider the number of people who do a lot of talking without any consideration for the listener. Words tumble out in heaps and cascade about the room. The listeners struggle to concentrate but after a time their attention wanes and they long for the end of the monologue. Their occasional efforts to interrupt or offer comment are swept away. Over a period of time, the victims of this word storm find strategies to avoid being pinned down by the hail of words by exchanging only fleeting remarks as they quickly pass by. Even if such people have something valuable to say, their inability to make the necessary connections with the listener, so essential to good communication, ensures that little transmission of ideas will take place.

The essence of effective verbal communication is that speakers have a receptive audience.

The power of words

Words can build up or destroy. They can float away upon the wind or find a resting place in people's minds and hearts. The power of words can be demonstrated with reference to two outstanding examples from recent history.

Example 1

The following advertisement was placed in the newspaper by the famous explorer Ernest Shackleton, when he was recruiting people for an expedition to the South Pole:

> Men wanted for hazardous journey. Small wages, bitter cold, long months of complete darkness, constant danger, safe return unlikely. Honour and recognition in case of success.

The response to the advertisement was overwhelming. Despite the gender bias contained within the wording, there are useful clues about the way in which the style of it has important implications for the spoken word.

- The text begins with a short, incisive statement, including an emotive adjective: 'hazardous'. If we were to say the statement out loud instead of writing it, we would probably emphasise the word hazardous, perhaps by using a slight inflection, lowering the pitch of the word or elongating the first syllable.

- The second sentence consists of short phrases which gather momentum: small wages/bitter cold/long months/complete darkness, ending with a clever twist: safe return <u>unlikely</u>. Again, we can imagine how, by contrast with the slow and deliberate opening sentence, the phrases in the second would snap out like shots from a gun, ending with a deliberate pause before the final word of the sentence: 'safe return... unlikely'.

■ The third sentence contains a mixture of sweet and bitter prospects: the possibility of honour and recognition cloaked in stark reality. The spoken version of the final sentence might be delivered in a measured, serious tone containing just a hint of gentle scepticism.

These words were written in a newspaper but offer some helpful insights into the way in which words can be used to convey a strong image to the listener, evoke an emotional response and (in this case) inspire action.

Example 2

The British Prime Minister, Winston Churchill, is often commended for his wartime speeches. Thus, when he declared 'We shall defend our island...' his voice dropped like a pebble down a well over the five words until the last word hits the bottom with a dull thud. Again, he growls... 'we shall <u>never</u> surrender!' in which he twists the word 'never' into 'naver' to emphasise it. Churchill practised and shaped the words before a major speech to ensure maximum impact. He knew, like many orators before him, that although words will be received in differing ways by an audience, if they are delivered with the appropriate tone and intonation, they can spur the majority to the desired forms of behaviour.

Words, then, are not to be handled casually, as their impact can have important consequences for the listener. Words used effectively can remain in our consciousness for a long time and influence our attitudes and priorities well into the future.

Penetrating words

Sticks and stones may break my bones but words can never hurt me. (Traditional rhyme)

It is difficult to think of a more ridiculous saying than the one above. Perhaps the original author was trying to convey that words could not do a person any physical damage or merely intended to provoke a reaction. Whatever the intention, words have had a powerful influence on generations of children and resulted in verbal bullying being treated less seriously than it ought.

Words are a powerful tool for carrying information, offering emotional support, accusing, directing, enticing, persuading and conveying hostility. There cannot be a single person reading this book who has not benefited from kind words or suffered from harsh ones. A parent's indictment can echo in a child's mind for years to come; a teacher's off-hand remark (quickly forgotten by the speaker) can confirm a pupil's worst fears or set in train an attitude of low self-esteem (where the pupils do not think much of themselves) or low self-concept (where the pupils are convinced that others do not think much of them). Although we all say things that we later regret, even our most heartfelt apology to the recipient of our torrent cannot fully atone for the damage caused.

Activity 1

People tend to use words as weapons when they are stressed, afraid or feeling insecure.

1. Make a list of three or four occasions in your life when you may tend to use harsh words unnecessarily.

2. Tick one or more of the following to explain your actions:
   - I was over-tired at the time.
   - I was overloaded with work at the time.
   - I felt ill and could not cope.
   - I thought that the person was trying to get at me.
   - I felt that I was being treated unfairly.
   - I knew that I deserved what was said.
   - I was scared.
   - I felt guilty.
   - I felt inadequate.

3. Discuss with a trusted colleague how you might change your behaviour. For instance:

- I could ensure that I went to bed at a sensible time.
- I could seek advice about improving my time management and spreading my workload.
- I could take time off when I was unfit instead of struggling nobly into work.
- I could take a less defensive view of peoples' motives.
- I could tell the person that I thought they were being unfair instead of bottling it up.
- I could admit that I was in the wrong and apologise.
- I could seek the support of others.
- I could set about making amends.
- I could sit down with a friend or senior colleague and list my strengths and attributes.

Communicating through talk

Speech communication is an activity unique to humans and is our chief means of expressing our thoughts and feelings, and of communicating with others. Indeed, it is difficult to imagine life without words, though people who have speaking or hearing difficulties find other means of communicating through signing. Although a small number of people suffer from ailments or brain disorders which prevent speech from taking place, and a few children elect to be mute for a period of time, there is an expectation that babies will gradually learn to speak. Deviation from this pattern is interpreted as unnatural and is a source of distress to parents.

Silverstein (1974) suggests that in order to be able to speak effectively, a person should possess six distinguishable levels of capacity:

Level 1
The ability to <u>hear</u> acoustic signals.

Level 2
Information about the sounds of the language (phonology).

Level 3

Information about the formation of sentences (syntax).

Level 4

Information about the meanings of words and combinations of words (lexicon).

Level 5

Knowledge about the world around (concept).

Level 6

A system of beliefs in order to evaluate the things that are heard.

- **Grammar** deals with the first four of these levels: hearing; interpreting sounds; understanding the composition of sentences; knowledge of vocabulary.

- Aspects of **concept and belief**, represented through the fifth and sixth levels, play an essential role in using and understanding the spoken word. Conceptual development allows words to be used meaningfully and intelligently. Beliefs are expressed through the use of words or formed as words are used to explore ideas, sharpen thinking and construct a viewpoint.

Talk needs to have an audience. Speech that involves only a speaker is like a river emptying its contents into the Dead Sea. When the words of the speaker are heard by the ears and mind of a listener who is receptive to their meaning, true communication may be said to be taking place. Both speaking and listening are necessary. Horner (1970) offers a useful analysis of communication through speech as involving a speaker who:

- encodes ideas into words;
- speaks the words;
- reinforces them according to conviction;
- transmits them to a listener;

and a listener who:

- hears what the speaker has said;
- decodes the words into received information;
- interprets their meaning in the light of experience;

■ reacts to the message received.

The speaker receives feedback from the listener which may or may not result in further conversation. If there is limited response from the listener, the verbal exchange is likely to end quite speedily, though sometimes the listener needs time to evaluate the content of each phrase, sentence and statement before responding. The eventual response may not be vocal but instead take the form of a body movement (such as a nod or shrug) though it is considered impolite in western countries to use casual body language at the expense of the spoken word.

> Speech may theoretically be classified into two extreme categories: one aiming at conveying information believed to be authentic; the other provocatively presenting a point of view or persuading a listener to change his mind or to coerce him into believing that which cannot be proved. (Horner, 1970)

Activity 2

In your work as a teacher, how much of your time is spent as a speaker and how much as a listener? Over the period of a day, consciously note when you speak and when you listen. Use the following categories as a guide:

Speaking	100%	75%	50%	25%	0%
Listening	0%	25%	50%	75%	100%

What are the implications for your job as a teacher?

Contexts for talk

Talk takes place in a thousand different settings: in homes, telephone boxes, debates, church services, space satellites and classrooms. It serves many purposes: sometimes formal and significant, sometimes casual and inconsequential. There are many synonyms for the word 'talk', including chat, gossip, natter, preach, prattle – which reinforce the multiplicity of opportunities for talking.

Talk is a skilful activity and important for learning

Effective communication requires an adequate grasp of vocabulary, clarity of purpose and an awareness of the impact our words have upon the listener. Talk is not like a hobby that can be done for its own sake; it is intended to have a purpose and provoke a reaction in the listener.

Different kinds of talk have to conform to different conventions

Sometimes the conventions are specified by the leader (such as a judge in court) or agreed by the participants (such as pupils performing some improvised drama). Sometimes the conventions emerge gradually as a result of the verbal interactions (such as when people from different cultures try to communicate); sometimes there is a well-established rule form which governs speech but has to be learned by every newcomer to the situation (such as young children starting school or in student discussions at college). Parents reinforce social conventions when they speak to their children:

- 'Please don't interrupt when I'm speaking.'
- 'Wait your turn.'
- 'Don't call out.'
- 'There's no need to shout.'

Variations in speech form can be recognised when the same two people meet in different relational settings. The light-hearted banter between colleagues at the staff room party are markedly different from a discussion about discipline problems in school or college between the same people sitting in the Head Teacher's office.

Although participants adopt appropriate patterns of talk, determined by the context, it is something of a mystery about how they know what to say, and when and how to say it. Different societies and social settings, including school and college situations, are founded upon an adherence to certain conventions; infractions cause alarm, disquiet, anger or resentment. A pupil who calls out a cheery greeting while walking into assembly may be reprimanded, whereas the same event at the end of the school day in the playground may receive approval. Edwards and Westgate (1994) draw attention to the fact that in many societies, children learn through imitating more experienced members of the group rather than being told how to do things. However, they note that in the classroom 'most lessons are verbal encounters orchestrated by the teacher' – a point that we shall focus on throughout succeeding chapters.

Activity 3

1. On a given day, note how many different individuals you speak to...

Fewer than 5 **Between 5 and 10** **Between 10 and 15**
More than 15

2. On the second day, note how often you speak to a small number of listeners at the same time (**fewer than 10**).
3. On the third day, note how often you speak to a large number of listeners at the same time (**more than 10**).
   - How does your speech vary according to the number of listeners?
   - What speech conventions operate in each case?

Speed of speech

When speech is <u>too fast</u>, words become distorted or too complicated for someone to absorb all the ideas contained within the verbal transmission. If speech is <u>too slow</u>, the impact is tedious and uninspiring, and the speaker gives the impression of being insecure or incompetent. Close friends, who have an intimate knowledge of one another's preferences, are able to exchange ideas with minimal speech patterns, such as the use of phrases like 'sort of...' or 'if you want...' or 'I'm easy'. Some people speak very quickly when they get excited or enthusiastic. Others deliberately slow down at key points in their speech to emphasise a point or to sound menacing.

Although it is important to speak at a consistent pace, the speed will vary according to circumstances. Generally, the larger the space, the slower the speed of speech needs to be. In a smaller room, when people are physically closer, it is possible to speak more rapidly and still be understood. On the other hand, if a person speaks too quickly for too long, it has a wearing effect upon an audience, who may respond by being restless, asking for clarification or becoming distracted.

We also need to differentiate between the process of speaking slowly when we leave slightly longer gaps and pauses between words and at the end of sentences, and when we say individual words slowly. Saying individual words slowly can be used to emphasise the word, but if strings of words are spoken too slowly, the overall impression can be wearisome.

Speech can be used in two ways:
1. **forming words and sentences to transmit information to listeners;**
2. **a formal, uninterrupted verbal presentation to an audience.**
   <u>Talking</u> or <u>speaking</u> takes place when words are used in exchanging meaning, enhancing understanding and communicating ideas.

The function of speech

Developing speech patterns that are comprehensible to a listener takes place over the first years of life at a basic level, but then continue to be refined as we meet new situations and enlarge our vocabulary and understanding of the world. Young children experiment with sounds, imitate their parents and siblings, use monosyllabic words in conjunction with hand signals, and gradually become aware that conventions of speech are locked in with order and sequence. Clumsy arrangements of words such as 'Me want go' are gradually replaced by 'I want to go home now' as adults help them to model the correct sentence structure and conform to agreed speech conventions. They learn, for instance, all the world of difference between 'The dog ate the bone' and 'The bone ate the dog'. They discover that if they interrupt adult speech, they are told to wait. They gradually understand the need to take turns and accommodate other people's ideas into their own thinking. Over time, they find out that listening to others is as important as giving their own opinions. Some learn these things quicker than others!

Word sequences also have a social dimension

Speech conventions vary from region to region, affected by dialect and local circumstances. People from outside an area can be effectively excluded from conversations if locals choose to lapse into dialect. Bilingual speakers can revert to their second language or move between languages if they wish to exercise control over a person in the group with knowledge of only one language. Group membership sometimes depends upon a knowledge of these conventions; any deviation from the accepted norms can lead to derision or exclusion. Children soon become aware that they have to conform if they want to be accepted by others. From the earliest time in school, children who are perceived as different in the way they speak or respond may be ostracised or be the target for unkind comments from their class-mates. Older children use the vocabulary of the day and loudly proclaim their interests by use of the latest vernacular or expressions, especially those which puzzle grown-ups! Accordingly, particular social settings influence the way we speak and behave.

Infant children have to learn that events often follow patterns that can be articulated and described. In school, teaching strategies are used to help pupils come to terms with sequencing by providing them with activities that require following directions for (say) recipes or mapwork or reinforcing their understanding through examining patterns of the day, calendar events and the procedures necessary to achieve particular outcomes. Younger pupils are encouraged to share the events of a weekend or special event as a means of helping them to convey accurately the unfolding and connected stages of a complex series of inter-dependent happenings. Older pupils have to deal with outcomes and changes which result from experimentation, choices and political decisions.

Children discover that making sense of statements relies on understanding previous ones

As young people mature, they learn to phrase sentences in order to reinforce the meaning and assist the listener to grasp the full implications of the words. Expressions commonly used include 'Let me put it another way' or 'If we view it from the other way around...' in an attempt to vary the speech sequences to facilitate fuller understanding. Gradually, children and young people recognise that effective speech assists communication.

Forms of talk

There are three basic forms of talk:

- Narration;
- Description;
- Explanation.

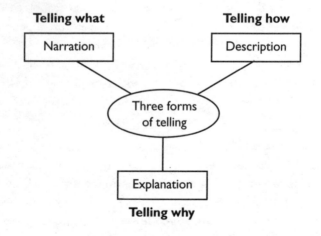

Figure 2 – *Telling what, how and why*

Narration: when the emphasis in speech is telling *what*.

Saying what happened necessitates putting things in time order, such as providing a sequence of events (for example from getting up to going to bed) or providing directions (for example following a science experiment). Narrative offers the listener the basic framework within which more elaborate describing and explaining can be located. Any attempt to provide too much detail or an elaborate justification for events without the narrative framework can lead to confusion, as the listener attempts to assimilate and interpret ideas without a structure within which to locate them.

In one of the Enid Blyton's stories Noddy argues, with remarkable logic, that when building a house it is sensible to put the roof on first in case it rains. Unfortunately, it is not possible to put on the roof without first laying a foundation and then constructing the walls. In the same way, to introduce the listener to specific detail without first establishing or building in a narrative framework, is likely to be counterproductive.

Description: when the emphasis in speech is telling *how*.

Whereas narrative sequences help to establish a framework of understanding, the ability to convey detail depends upon the speaker's ability to describe situations in such a way that the words used help the listener to gain a mental picture of the circumstances or events. While narrative is dependent upon the careful use of appropriate verbs (went, proceeded, discovered, continued, facilitated and so on) descriptive talk relies on imaginative use of adjectives, comparisons and symbolism to achieve the desired end. For instance, a <u>narration</u> about the start of a school day might look like this:

> 'The teacher opened the classroom door, entered the room, gazed around the class, sat on her chair, opened the register and called out the names in alphabetical order.'

Whereas a <u>description</u> would assume that the sequence was known and be more concerned with providing word pictures for the listener. Thus:

> 'The nervous teacher peered around the classroom door, gazed with large eyes around the class of faces, some of them sullen, others eager. She sat on the edge of her chair; opened the register with trembling hands and, avoiding eye contact with pupils, feebly called out the names of the class in alphabetical order'.

The descriptive passage offers more detail than the simple narrative and gives the listener (or reader) some insights into how things took place and paints in key actions and reactions which allows the listener to catch something of the emotional tension and atmosphere of the event. An effective description leads to questions about why it happened in the way it did, what caused the circumstances to arise, and what happened next. Skilful speakers (and writers) combine narrative and description in such a way that it induces interest in finding out more about the situation. For instance, see how this passage raises your interest level:

> *The moon was up but often obscured; clouds drifted swiftly across her face; it was a cold morning, past one o'clock. Josephs was at his window, standing tiptoe on his stool. Thoughts course one another across his broken heart as fast as the clouds flew past the moon's face, but whatever their nature, the sting was now out of them. The bitter sense of wrong and cruelty was there, but blunted. Fear was nearly extinct, for hope was dead.*
>
> **(from Charles Read: It Is Never Too Late To Mend)**

The descriptive character of this passage can be appreciated in its own right, but unless we know the place of this episode in the story, questions inevitably arise in our minds:

- What is happening now?
- What has happened before?
- What happens next?

There are also unexplained questions about the reasons for this unusual circumstance:

- Why is Josephs up at night?
- Why is he staring out of the window?
- Why is there such a sense of foreboding?

These and other questions demand explanation if the picture is to be made complete.

Explanation: when the emphasis in speech is telling *why*.

Wragg (1993) suggests that 'explaining something clearly to a pupil lies at the very centre of a good teacher's professional repertoire'. He emphasises that explanations may take a variety of forms but always fulfil the purpose of helping others to understand something better. Wragg underlines the point that an effective explanation seeks to see matters from the learner's perspective and involve pupils in the process through offering them opportunities for dialogue and discussion. Dean (1992) warns against using unsuitable terms or over-complex sentence structures when explaining. Dean suggests that explanations are likely to fall into one of five categories based on a pupil's questions:

- what to do next;
- where to find something;
- queries about the work;
- checking the correctness of work;
- permission to do something.

Ideally, explanations should be based on the types of questions that pupils ask and that the teacher anticipates they may ask (Kerry, 1998). In practice, teachers often explain procedures for task completion and as a means of monitoring progress rather than as a response to pupils' questions.

Activity 4

1. Tape record a 30 minute teaching session in which you spend time talking to the class.

2. Listen to the recording and note the amount of time you use **narrative**, **description** and **explanation**, and where you combined them.

3. The following day, ask a random sample of two or three pupils to tell you what they remember from the lesson.

4. Which of the forms of talk were most memorable for them?

Combining narrative, description and explanation

Whereas narrative emphasises a sequence of events, and description paints word pictures for the listener, explanation demonstrates the relationship between one event and another; that is, it offers reasons for certain things happening in the way they do and what causes things to take place.

For instance, a **narrative** account of someone getting ready for work in the morning might mention washing, dressing, going downstairs, breakfast, leaving the house, catching the bus and so on.

A **descriptive** account might refer to the person's sleepy looks, the colour of the jacket, the speed at which breakfast was eaten and the race to catch the bus. Neither narrative nor description, however, offer any explanation about why people need to use the bathroom first thing in the morning, the factors influencing choice of jacket, the size of breakfast or the reasons for catching public transport rather than taking the car. For those who have experienced this situation themselves, the explanation is probably unnecessary. They know that failure to use the bathroom will lead to discomfort; they are aware that the day's programme influences the choice of jacket and that the size of breakfast will affect the rate of metabolism; they have experienced the moral dilemma of whether or not to take the car; they have rushed to be on time, conscious of the consequences that attend lateness.

We cannot, however, assume that our listeners will have the knowledge, understanding or experience to be able to evaluate an existing situation. There are many instances in which the significance of events is lost on the listener due to inexperience, unfamiliarity with conventions, innocence or ignorance. Four year-olds do not normally think of the impact of weather conditions upon the harvest when they are asked by a parent to select a favourite cereal. Few nine year-olds will query the purpose of holding a school assembly; not many fifteen year-olds will demand an explanation for having a prime minister at the head of the government. Only when teachers provoke pupils' interest about things they take for granted will most of them begin to probe and question for themselves.

Once an explanation has been offered, pupils may not be satisfied with what they hear

Young children are prone to ask a lot of questions once their interest is aroused if allowed to do so. Primary teachers often find that their attempts to explain apparent inequalities or unfairness results lead to pupil indignation. Young people can be idealistic, even unreasonable, as they come to grips with difficult issues and dilemmas. The wise teacher is sensitive to the kinds of reactions which explanations can engender in their pupils. Teachers do not have the luxury of the harassed parents who were heard telling their children: 'Never mind <u>why</u>; just do what we say'!

Explanation offers opportunities for many kinds of learning:

- Problem solving in which cause and effect is significant.
- Examining the impact of actions upon others.
- The ethical issues underpinning events.

A combination of the three forms (narration, description and explanation) provides a powerful teaching and learning tool for pupils and teachers at all stages of education.

Activity 5

1. Write down about five phrases, normally heard only in school settings, that might mystify a stranger.

2. Write an alternative for each phrase in 'friendly-speak'.

Chapter 2

Clarity of speech

If only for the children's sake, we should avoid the worst vocal faults by paying some attention to voice production. The minimum requirement should be a voice that is not unpleasant to listen to.

(Sansom, 1978)

Effective verbal communication is a two-way process involving speaking and listening, exchange of information and the development of a shared understanding. In Chapter 1 we considered the power of words, the contexts for talk and the forms of talk used in the majority of verbal encounters. Another important factor in communicating with listeners is to ensure that the spoken voice is of good quality and that speakers are fully utilising their abilities. An untrained voice from an unprepared speaker will considerably reduce the impact of what is said, regardless of how interesting the subject content may be. This chapter focuses on ways to enhance your ability to communicate what needs to be said.

Good health and speaking

State of health is an important factor in any form of public speaking. Good health means more than guarding against the coughs and colds that damage the voice and spoil the presentation. The act of speaking in front of an audience is often physically demanding and mentally exhausting. The possession of a good constitution enables the brain to work more efficiently, the body to withstand the demands placed upon it, and the mind to cope with the rigours of addressing your listeners.

Those who are serious about public speaking should consider themselves as much in training as an athlete preparing for a series of races. Regular sleep, a sensible diet and a positive attitude to people and life in general, are prerequisites for giving and gaining the most from time spent in front of an audience.

The use of the voice

Speech consists of shaping and controlling the breath which is made to vibrate as it passes through the gap between the vocal chords. It is moulded into vowel sounds depending upon the shape of the mouth and articulated into consonants by holding back the flow of air in different ways. Phonemes are the smallest speech parts which combine to form syllables. Syllables are made into words which combine to produce phrases. Continuous speech is divided into phrases, separated by pauses to allow for a further intake of air and giving expression to the spoken word.

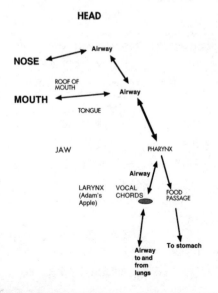

Figure 3 – Speech Parts

Teachers' voices

Teachers use their voices a lot. From first thing in the morning they are speaking to their pupils, liaising with colleagues or talking to other adults. Sometimes they speak for a considerable length of time, such as explaining something to a class or taking an assembly; sometimes the exchanges are short and concise, such as when dealing with an instance of misbehaviour; sometimes, the voice has to be loud, such as during a large space lesson (such as games); sometimes, soft and gentle, such as making comments when hearing a child read. Fontana (1994) summarises the position:

> The voice is the teacher's main line of communication to the class.
> It is a medium through which the teacher exercises the majority of
> managerial functions. Obviously it should be used to communicate
> clearly and with sufficient volume.

On occasions anger, fear, uncertainty or frustration cause teachers to misuse their voices, creating stress and strain on the vocal chords. Teachers who persist in overworking their voices may not only suffer physical damage but induce exhaustion and ill-health.

Activity 6

Make a deliberate effort to listen to your own voice throughout a day. Note the times when it becomes strained...

1. Put in order of priority the circumstances that created the strain:

- I spoke too quickly because of time constraints.
- I was angry and lost control of my voice.
- I was trying to make myself heard above the noise.
- I spoke continuously for too long.
- I used a higher pitch to make myself heard.
- Other reasons (note).

2. What did you notice about your own sense of well-being during those occasions?

3. Note down things that you might have done. For instance:

- spoken more concisely;

- kept things in proportion instead of losing my head;
- gained the pupils' attention by a different means before I commenced speaking;
- included short pauses between my blocks of speech;
- tried strengthening my voice rather than shouting.

Taking care of the voice

The voice is to the teacher what muscles are to the athlete. Although it would be possible to teach without a voice, the task would become difficult and demanding. Despite the urgent need to take care of their voices, it is surprising that so few teachers appear to take the time and trouble to do so. While trainee teachers are told how to teach subjects, develop classroom management skills and think like professionals, training courses often seem to assume that voice quality can be left to chance. Unless there is a particularly severe problem with classroom communication concerning, say, audibility or tone, most student teachers do not receive specific help from their tutors. Yet even experienced teachers who have no immediate voice production problems are storing up trouble if they do not take good care of this prime asset. All teachers are capable of improving their voice quality if they spend a little time and effort on training, as well as schools saving money that has to be paid out due to absenteeism. Pupils benefit from the continuity that comes from being taught by the same teacher instead of stand-in staff. Voice care pays dividends for everyone.

There are a number of simple exercises which help the voice to 'warm up' for speaking. They can be done easily, away from public view, helping to ensure that the voice parts (throat, tongue, lips and so on) are in the right condition to support the major task of communicating with pupils and other adults. The exercises can be divided into two main sorts: 1) Relaxing the muscles; 2) Keeping the main speech parts supple.

Relaxing the muscles

The parts of the body associated with producing speech contain muscles which need to be kept in good condition if voice production is to be at its best. Hitchman (1977) suggests that there are two main causes of voice problems: excessive muscular tension and poor breathing for speaking.

> *Excessive muscular tension tends to force up the pitch of the voice. One concomitant is increased and unvaried volume; another is harsh, strident tone which can result in vocal fatigue and strain... and wear and tear on the pupils' nerves.*

Poor breathing results from having a negative attitude towards the task in hand, leading to a slumped posture, raised shoulders, elbows cramping the ribs and subsequent muscular tension. Good breathing is assisted by learning to relax through being well informed about what has to be done and approaching the task confidently. Drawing steady breaths through the nose and exhaling slowly through the mouth slows the heart rate and concentrates the mind. It is also useful to spend a little time gently massaging the face and neck at the start of the day or before you begin talking.

Keeping the main speech parts supple

Supple lips and tongue are essential for effective speaking. The lips can be loosened by saying words using a normal tone in which a consonant is followed by a vowel, such as: '...mini mini mini...maxi maxi maxi...' gradually increasing the speed while maintaining a steady sound. Similarly, use of a tongue twister can assist in loosening the main speech parts. For instance: '...the wiggly weasel wandered away from the whispering warren...'.

If you try saying these word strings without emphasising any of the syllables, including the letter 's' sound, you will have to exercise much tighter breath control. If you exaggerate the 'w' sound, stretching your mouth as you do so, your lips have to work much harder and you use more air in speaking.

Activity 7

1. Practise saying the words '...shy shepherds sheltered the shifty sheep...' slowly and deliberately; mentally follow the position of your lips and tongue. Feel the pursed lips position when you sound

out 'sh', the open mouth for the 'she' of shepherds, the tightness of lips for the 'p' of shepherd, the change of position of the tongue in 'shifty sheep'.

2. Moving your lips freely, say the well known rhyme out loud: a) very slowly; b) at normal conversation speed; c) at the pace of a horse racing commentator...

'Peter Piper picked a peck of pickled pepper; a peck of pickled pepper, Peter Piper picked; if Peter Piper picked a peck of pickled pepper, where's the peck of pickled pepper Peter Piper picked?'

3. Spend a few moments gently massaging your face and neck, stretching your lips and circling your tongue. Repeat 2) above and notice the difference in the smooth flow of words.

To loosen the lips and tongue, it is important to exaggerate the sounds and put them to the front of the mouth rather than towards the back (which gives a plummy sound to words) without straining or altering your pitch unduly. Combining simple word exercises with relaxed muscles makes a surprising difference in preparing to speak clearly and minimising voice strain.

Breathing

One of the most important aspects of voice projection relates to satisfactory breath control. Good breath control depends upon approaching what we are doing in a positive frame of mind so that we do not feel tense and anxious, correct posture to avoid cramping the lungs and careful control of the flow of air from the lungs to the mouth. Improvement of lung capacity can take place gradually by practising simple exercises which will assist development and facilitate good breath control.

The following section is concerned with describing some techniques to help improve lung health and thereby improve fitness for speaking. It is, however, important to remember that carrying out these exercises will not, of themselves, transform our ability to speak. They must be carried out in the knowledge that in the same way as putting top grade petrol into a rusty old engine will not guarantee a safe journey to the desired destination, so improving lung quality and breath control will not ensure effective verbal communication if the many other factors described elsewhere in this book are neglected.

Learning how to breathe correctly is fundamental to every speech act

It helps to think of our lungs as a large, hollow, pear-shaped object. Without air the lungs are similar to a deflated balloon (though in fact the lungs are never entirely empty of air). As we breath in through our noses (inhale), part of the balloon fills with gas and inflates; as we breathe out (exhale) the balloon deflates and grows flatter. However, whereas a balloon will normally deflate fully and inflate to the point of bursting, our lungs never fully deflate and certainly do not reach their capacity as there are areas which remain under-used and reduce the lungs' capacity. For speaking, these neglected areas of the lungs need to be brought into use.

Air needs to travel into every part of the lungs if they are to inflate fully. If the sides and lower areas of the lungs remain under-used, we lose a lot of potential air and have to breath more often to provide the air our bodies requires for speaking. Regular exercise to utilise the lungs' potential capacity provides the foundation for improving breath control and tonal quality.

Learning to relax is essential to effective voice production

It is useful to contrast the way in which nervous young children react when they are singing and a politician responds to tough questioning by a television interviewer. Whereas young children seem to snatch air from around them by raising their shoulder height level with their ears as they struggle to find sufficient breath, the politician sits or stands in a relaxed but upright position with loose shoulders, breathing through the nose and allowing the regular flow of air from the lungs to carry the sound of the words. The child becomes tired from the physical exertion and uses up more energy replenishing the expended air than for producing sound with it. The politician seems relatively untroubled by the experience. When people are under severe pressure, they can lose their voice completely, often because they forget to breathe properly or their muscles are so tense that much of the oxygen from breathing is used to sustain vital body functions. Under the worst conditions, people feel dizzy and may even collapse.

Activity 8

1. Stand in front of a long mirror and breathe in and out normally; watching the physical position of your body as you do so.

2. Take a much deeper breath.

■ Do your shoulders rise when you do so?

■ Do your muscles tense?

If so, you are not breathing in the most effective way and are using only a limited area of your lungs.

3. With shoulders still and body relaxed, practise breathing correctly so that air travels into your lower lungs as well as into the upper chest region.

4. Standing upright, with your feet comfortably apart for balance, practise breathing gradually and deeply (not sniffing in hard) in front of the mirror for up to a minute each day until you can breathe deeply without moving your shoulders.

■ You will need to resist the tendency to lift your shoulders as air is channelled to the lower parts of your lungs.

After a surprisingly short period of time, your breath will travel from where it is stored (the lungs) to where it is needed for sound (the throat and mouth) without the strain of excessive body movement.

Volume control

In an attempt to speak louder, we often force our voices without the breath to support what we are saying. Rodenburg (1992) describes this when she speaks about ways in which our voices may become 'trapped'. Perhaps as a result of nerves, insecurity or a feeling that we need to make an impact upon our listeners, we strain at the vocal chords and use the small amount of air in our throats rather than the considerable volume of air available in our lungs to carry the sound of our words. Our efforts to speak louder can be compared to a driver pressing the accelerator pedal down hard to the floor rather than change to a lower gear. The engine makes an unnatural sound, exhaust fumes cloud the air and the vehicle, despite its many protests, painfully reaches the desired speed, whereupon the driver relaxes back into the seat, eases the grip on the steering wheel and begins to breathe easily again. The damage to the engine is small and not immediately obvious, but over time, the wear and tear will result in expensive damage. So it is with our voices. A relaxed, unhurried yet purposeful voice, carried with controlled breathing to the lips and beyond, will offset this unnecessary yet common speech failing.

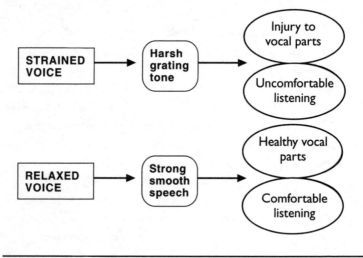

Figure 4 – *Volume control*

The following activities (2.4 and 2.5) will assist in developing lung capacity and giving us more control over the flow of air to support speech. They can be practised almost anywhere, any time, but are best performed in a warm (but not hot) room. It will take time to feel comfortable with the exercises, so it is important not to hurry and take account of your general state of health in determining how much you can manage.

Activity 9

Stage 1

Either standing still or walking along at a gentle pace, breathe in steadily through your nose for a slow count of four, hold for a count of four, and release air through your mouth over a count of four. Speak the numbers out loud. Remember to speak plainly and exaggerate the use of your lips and tongue. Repeat this a few times, remembering to stay relaxed and unhurried. Breath regularly and steadily; do not sniff hard or breathe in any way which strains your body.

Stage 2

Breath in for a count of four, then breathe out and expel the air in one go. Repeat this.

Stage 3

Breathe normally for a few seconds to settle yourself.

Stage 4

Now breathe in for four, hold for four, and release the air more slowly over a count of eight. Repeat a few times. Don't tense your muscles or or lift your shoulders. If a count of eight causes you any distress, return to 1) above and begin the exercise afresh.

Stage 5

Breathe normally for a minute to restore your body's equilibrium.

Stage 6

If the above stages have been accomplished comfortably, you may wish to increase the number of counts for the exhalation. That is, breathe out for a count of ten, twelve, even sixteen, as you become used to the exercise.

Stand still and relaxed with your feet comfortably apart. Spend a few minutes going through Activity 2.4 to gain the necessary control over your inhalation and exhalation. Breathe normally for a minute, stand still and relaxed with your feet comfortably apart. Take sensible precautions to ensure that you don't strain or overdo the exercise. Do not hurry or use jerky movements.

Activity 10

Stage 1

With feet apart and hands on hips, breathe in deeply for a count of four, exhale for a count of eight. Repeat.

Stage 2

Breathe in for a count of four while bowing your body forward from the waist. Exhale slowly for a count of eight as your body resumes its upright position. Repeat.

Stage 3

Breathe in for a count of four while gently leaning your body to the right. If you feel that you may fall, use your extended right arm to lean against a solid object. Breathe out for a count of eight. Repeat.

Stage 4

As in 3) but leaning to the left. Remember to breathe out slowly and regain your upright position gradually.

Stage 5

Begin from the start, using <u>different counts</u> (ten, twelve, sixteen) as appropriate. Don't spend too long on this exercise or you may tire. Always take time out to breathe normally and regain your equilibrium between repeats.

Activity 2.5 is useful for driving air into the areas of your lungs which are under-used. Stage 2 of the exercise deliberately cramps the front of the lungs and forces the body to store air in the less frequently used back parts, with a gradual increase in the lung's usable storage capacity. Similarly, leaning to the left extends the area on the right side, and vice versa.

Always take sensible precautions with any physical exercise. If in doubt, consult a doctor first.

Although the activities will not create healthy lungs out of unhealthy ones they will, if used regularly, enhance your lung capacity and your ability to control the air needed for speaking. If you have any doubts about your fitness or the suitability of these exercises, always consult the appropriate professional before commencing. There are also numerous keep-fit programmes which may be helpful in maintaining your body's general well-being.

Pacing

The <u>pace</u> of speaking is not only about the number of words spoken in a given time. It is also determined by the extent to which a speaker engages the listener, both mentally and emotionally.

At its simplest, the pace of speech can be described numerically by counting the number of words uttered per minute. However, adjusting the pace of talking is more complex than can be represented through a number and will vary according to circumstances, including the type of audience, the complexity of the information and the size of the room. A well informed audience will normally be able to handle a faster flow of words, though very young pupils or elderly listeners will not always be able to assimilate and process ideas quickly. Complex information usually needs to be presented more carefully than familiar material. The pace of speech in larger rooms should be reduced slightly as there may be problems with echoes if words are uttered too quickly. The pace may also have to be adjusted in crowded rooms as the sound is absorbed by the bodies present.

If the pace is too rapid and the ideas too numerous, the listener will have insufficient time to handle the flow of ideas and either become distracted, annoyed or pick up only part of the intended meaning. If the pace is too slow, it is likely to create impatience or boredom.

There are also emotional factors to take into account when considering an appropriate pace. For words to convey a message, they must have authority and conviction. Speakers who are technically efficient but fail to touch the hearts or spirits of the listeners will rarely gain the attention and response they hope for. Horner (1970) underlines this when he asserts that '...emotion is still the driving force of human communication...'. For instance, it would be entirely inappropriate to hurry through a resumé of someone's life during their funeral service, whereas teachers may speak very rapidly when reminding their class of familiar procedures such as keeping things tidy or remembering their homework.

Nelson-Jones (1986) suggests that the atmosphere is influenced by the messages that our voices carry during a conversation. He offers a list of desirable qualities, an amended form of which is given below:

Table 1

Desirable qualities for voices (after Nelson-Jones, 1986)

- *appropriate volume*
- *a reasonable pace*
- *expressive emphases*
- *a natural tone*
- *clear enunciation*
- *lightly accented*
- *firm speech*
- *use of pauses and silences*

Maintaining an appropriate pace means that listeners will be allowed some thinking time. Speakers must attend to the speed at which they deliver their words and the reaction of the listeners. Through pauses in delivery and, in some cases, breaking off from speaking, they can involve their audience through eye contact, visual aids and, where appropriate, allowing opportunities for questions and comment.

We cannot assume that because the audience is attentive, people are necessarily thinking about what is being said, nor that inattentiveness means that they are not listening.

Delivery

Speaking is not, of course, simply a case of articulating words of a particular kind in a particular order. Our words need to carry conviction and be transmitted with appropriate enthusiasm and conviction if our listeners are to be satisfied. There are five factors that are important in enhancing the quality and impact made by your speaking:

1. Pitch

2. Inflection

3. Emphasis

4. Articulation

5. Rhythm

Pitch

Pitch depends principally upon the amount of air expelled from the lungs through the vocal chords. An increase in the volume of air leads to raised pitch; a decrease to a lowering of pitch. A higher pitch is, under normal circumstances, more penetrating than a lower one, though over-use of a raised pitch leads to fatigue and (as far as pupils are concerned) an annoying intrusion. It is important to retain strict control over air supply as excitement can result in a gradual and unintended raising of the voice pitch. On the other hand, a low pitch does not carry words as far and may, in a large space, cause difficulty for those at the back.

Sometimes, nerves and anxiety lead to a lowering of pitch due to the small amount of air transmitted across the vocal chords. In extreme circumstances, it is not unknown for someone to lose their voice completely during times of acute pressure. It is better to try and maintain a natural speaking tone, using good breathing techniques and a relaxed posture. The eventual vocal tone should be reassuring and familiar rather than harsh and disturbing. Although the pitch should be kept in the middle range for most of the time we are speaking, some variation can be used to create interest in the listeners or for particular purposes such as when we are reading aloud.

Activity 11

1. Write down three or four expressions that you regularly use with pupils during the day.

2. Say them out loud in a high, normal and low pitch.

3. What differences do you notice about:

- the volume;
- the effect on your throat;
- the conviction with which you can convey meaning?

Inflection

Where the change from one pitch to another is made in passing from one word or syllable to another, it is termed inflection. It is obvious that there are many thousands of possible inflections available to speakers to reflect their mood and the effect they wish their words to have on the listeners. A good grasp of inflection will help a speaker to be more interesting to listen to and avoid the tedium which results from talking at a constant pitch.

Activity 12

1. Practise saying a familiar rhyme such as <u>Ten Green Bottles</u>, using voice inflections to enliven an otherwise uninspiring piece.

2. Repeat using a sombre tone.

3. Repeat using an enthusiastic tone.

4. How many other inflections can you introduce to give fresh meaning to familiar words?

Emphasis

Emphasis (or stress) of a word or phrase can take place using any pitch. Although a variation in inflection can, of itself, emphasise the significant word or phrase, there are two other strategies available to speakers: a) pausing before or after the significant word or phrase; b) saying the word or phrase at a different speed from the rest of the sentence. It is not advisable to over-use any of these techniques but rather to use to emphasis sparingly to create the maximum impact.

Activity 13

1. Read the following familiar part of the Christmas story, putting an emphasis in the correct place:

> *And the shepherds came with haste and found Mary and Joseph and the baby lying in a manger.*

If read without a pause, it sounds as if all three were lying in the manger. Only if read with a pause after the word Joseph, does it make sense. Try it again.

2. Read the stanza from Wordsworth's well-known poem, emphasising key words and using pauses to gain maximum effect:

> *For oft when on my couch I lie in vacant or in pensive mood/ they flash upon that inward eye/ which is the bliss of solitude/ and then my heart with pleasure fills/ and dances with the daffodils.*

Examples of how pitch, inflection and emphasis may be used in different teaching contexts will appear throughout the rest of this book. Gaining greater awareness of these three elements should result in improved speech quality.

Articulation

Articulation is an essential element of effective verbal communication. Young children are sometimes so excited that they gabble away, eyes blazing, arms waving, and completely inarticulate to the bewildered adult. Teenagers can be slovenly and speak in such a loose manner that words are indecipherable; the adult's polite request to hear it again is met with a 'never mind, it doesn't matter', which makes the situation even more frustrating. Adults can be inarticulate when they are nervous, anxious, upset or in a hurry.

Some speakers are difficult to follow because they mispronounce words, speak too rapidly so that words run into one another, or allow their voices to fall away at the end of each phrase. A good speaker makes sure that each sound is clear and easily heard by listeners. An audience will quickly tire and be far less inclined to sympathise with what is being said if people have to expend energy straining to hear.

Rodenburg (1992) stresses the importance of keeping the face, jaw, tongue and palate in good order to produce good quality speaking and maximise the likelihood of clear and natural speech. In doing so, we should aim at getting energetic speech without loudness. Rodenburg argues that vigorous speech comes partly from breath force, but also from strength of articulation. It is not dependent on volume. 'The aim in achieving clear speech is economy, efficiency and effortlessness in articulation.'

A consistent volume is particularly important if we are working with sensitive children who may react adversely to over-zealous speech.

Activity 14

Practise your articulation by saying the major-general's lines from Gilbert and Sullivan's <u>Pirates of Penzance</u>, remembering to free your cheek, lips and tongue before doing so:

I am the very model of a modern major-general/I've information vegetable, animal and mineral/I know the kings of England and can quote the facts historical/From Marathon to Waterloo in order categorical/I've very well acquainted, too, with matters mathematical/ I understand equations, both the simple and quadratical/About binomial theorems I'm teeming with a lot of news/With many cheerful facts about the square on the hypotenuse.

Rhythm

Rhythmic speech is easily recognised but not easily achieved or defined. It depends upon a combination of factors:

- **stress** (or emphasis) – when we use more breath to emphasise a word or syllable.

- **intonation** – the rise and fall in the pitch of the voice during normal speaking (see earlier).

- **articulation** (or enunciation or diction) – in which consonants are used to interrupt the flow of air and create word sounds (see earlier).

- **length** – the variety of length of sounds and syllables found in the English language; they can, of course, be deliberately extended for effect.

- **pace** – the rate of talking (see earlier).

- **pause** – created naturally due to the structure of sentences and deliberately for emphasis.

■ **phrasing** – when groups of words are used which fit together naturally.

Ideal rhythmic speech is achieved through maintaining ease of chest movement that facilitates flexible voice use, well co-ordinated phrases and sentences, and a smooth, natural and well-controlled delivery. The acquisition of rhythmic speech requires perseverance and determination but once achieved can transform the ordinary into something special.

The first rule for a teacher to observe in his classroom talking is to keep the normal rhythm of his speaking. This is vital to the clear projection of meaning and to easy, unstrained listening and instant comprehension. (Hitchman, 1977)

Confidence in speaking

Many inexperienced teachers, and a surprising number who have been teaching for many years, suffer from a lack of confidence which affects their ability to speak clearly and with the necessary conviction to convince their listeners that what they have to say is worth hearing. Student teachers, faced for the first time with a class of their own, describe the anxiety and, in some cases, gripping fear, that envelopes them when they face an audience of pupils. Linklater (1976) argues that 'blocked emotions are the fundamental obstacle to a free voice', and every student teacher knows that despite advice from tutors and books like this one, anxiety can drain both their stamina and ability to think straight. Unless emotion is properly under control, teachers blunder on in a kind of numb state, hearing their own voices, but feeling detached from reality. The end of the lesson cannot come soon enough.

Although Linklater's advice is sound, a great deal of perseverance and effort is needed before anxiety can be brought under control. It is first of all important to recognise the source of anxiety, which can arise due to a number of fear factors.

Table 2

Some sources of anxiety in speaking

- *fear of being humiliated;*
- *fear of being unable to cope;*
- *fear of getting in a tangle part way through;*
- *fear of antagonising your listeners;*
- *fear of boring your listeners;*
- *fear of losing control;*
- *fear of misjudging the time available;*
- *fear of failure.*

Bostock (1994) offers some helpful advice in dealing with fear:

- Use nerves positively as a stimulus rather than a suppressant.
- Prepare thoroughly.
- Show enthusiasm for your subject.
- Think positively about your audience.
- Maintain a good posture and breath freely.
- Enjoy the experience.

The importance of confidence in speaking is such that some comment on Bostock's points is merited.

Using nerves positively

Some people seem nerveless, but most of us suffer from some form of anxiety on occasions when we speak to an audience. Nerves can result in one of two outcomes:

- we become seized up and unable to function properly;
- we use the nervous energy as a spur to meeting the challenge head-on.

The second option is obviously the ideal one. To achieve it, we need to ameliorate the effect of our nerves by being well-informed about the topic, adequately rehearsing key points and seeking advice from more experienced practitioners beforehand.

Preparing thoroughly

Thorough preparation is not only concerned with knowing what we are talking about, but being clear about what is expected from us, anticipating questions and queries, and thinking through the way we will present material. There is nothing more reassuring than having confidence in what we know.

Showing enthusiasm

It is difficult to falsify enthusiasm. However, if we are not particularly keen on what we are doing, it is worth trying to convince ourselves that it is actually very interesting and that we are really pleased to have the opportunity to teach it. One way or another we have to ensure that when we interact with our audience, they are inspired rather than depressed by our presentation. Their positive reaction to our enthusiastic manner will help us communicate even more effectively as our confidence grows.

Thinking positively

Very few audiences find delight in destroying a speaker. Even problem classes contain a majority who are anxious to learn and want to support their teacher. It will help our confidence if we adopt a positive view of our listeners and convince ourselves that they want to hear what we say.

Enjoying the experience

The suggestion that doing something which creates anxiety should be enjoyed may seem a little odd, but it is good advice. The opportunity to address an audience is a worthwhile activity in its own right; relatively few people have such a privilege. We should take full advantage of it and treat each encounter as a step towards our goal of being an effective verbal communicator.

No-one will know that you are feeling anxious unless you disclose it.

Activity 15

Try reading the four lines of Gray's well known poem, <u>Elegy Written In A Country Churchyard</u>, emphasising key words and phrases. Imagine how you might make the maximum impact on an audience of:

a) eight year old primary pupils;

b) a group of elderly retired people.

The curfew tolls the nell of parting day;
The lowing herd winds slowly o'er the lea;
The ploughman homeward plods his weary way
And leaves the world to darkness and to me.

It may be that your delivery to the eight year-olds was more sparkling, with variations in pitch and emphasis of words such as day or herd or darkness. As you spoke the lines out loud, you may have seen the children in your mind's eye, imagined their response as you stressed parts of the stanza, or even found yourself using body language in front of your invisible audience to ensure that you retained their attention. Perhaps your delivery to the elderly folk was louder and a little more sombre. You may have emphasised the final word in each line or extended the vowel sounds in words like curfew and slowly, or made more pronounced mouth movements in your desire to ensure that you communicated with the audience, some of whom might have reduced hearing. Your delivery will, to some extent, be governed by the context in which you speak, in particular the composition of the audience.

Loss of voice quality

Loss of voice quality can occur in four ways.

Maintaining a high pitch

Although using a higher pitch will catch the listeners' attention initially, if it is used with a tense throat to create a sharp sound, it will be very unpleasant to listen to. Words come jumping out of the mouth like shots from an old blunderbuss rifle, hurting the ears and damaging the target. Over time, their impact diminishes as listeners learn to 'take cover' as the pepper of words scream overhead. It pays to ease into our words,

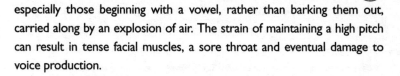

especially those beginning with a vowel, rather than barking them out, carried along by an explosion of air. The strain of maintaining a high pitch can result in tense facial muscles, a sore throat and eventual damage to voice production.

Strings of words that undulate in volume

When someone tries to talk loudly all the time, some words in the sentence come out forcefully and others more limply, leading to a situation in which the listener's ear is stunned by the sound of the loud words and straining to hear the others. The speaker's voice sounds like the engine of a car when it is started in the morning, as the motorist 'revs' up, then allows it to idle for a moment, before revving again. Contrast this to the well tuned, warm engine which maintains a regular, consistent and reassuring sound. We should aim to achieve the luxury car status with our voice production rather than sound like the old banger on a cold winter's morning!

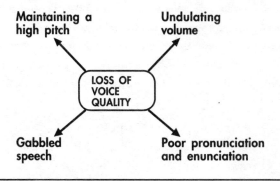

Figure 5 – Factors affecting voice quality

The tendency to gabble

It is one thing to speak forcefully when we have control of our breathing and the words glide out from our mouths towards their intended target. It is quite another thing to get carried away with the wonders of what we are saying and gradually get more and more animated as the volume increases and reaches a crescendo of words spurting out like hailstones. Listeners are bombarded with a multitude of sounds, words, ideas and questions that wear down their resistance until they become subdued and unresponsive or start to respond irritably, perhaps even starting to speak loudly themselves, adding to the cacophony. Meanwhile, our enthusiastic speaker continues regardless, chin in the air, arms gesticulating, producing an increasing torrent of verbiage that few people can follow or comprehend.

Poor pronunciation and enunciation

Some letter sounds are badly enunciated, leading to speech which is difficult to follow. For instance, the following are common speech failings which can make speaking difficult to follow:

- substituting a 'th' with a 'v' or with an 'f' – for instance, wever instead of weather; fink instead of think.
- creating a silent vowel – such as losing the 't' of repeated to make repea(t)ed.
- flabby lip movement, thereby losing the letter -g from the ends of words, such as talkin' instead of talking.

Although different dialects lead to certain inflections which cause single consonant and digraph sounds to be distorted or lost, it is worth persevering to eliminate excessive variations and concentrate on improving both the production of sounds (pronunciation) and the clarity with which they are translated into words (enunciation).

Good communicators do not need to rely on a high pitch or constant changes in volume or gabbling. To make ourselves heard clearly, it is essential to maintain a disciplined approach to talking: to breath naturally, relaxing the body and (especially) the face, neck and shoulders, to release words in the middle register, and to ensure that they leave our mouth at a rate that will allow listeners to hear, interpret, and reflect on what is being said.

Care over vocabulary

A person who uses an impressive vocabulary is usually admired or despised. It can be intimidating to speak to someone who uses terms and expressions that you have never heard or only have a vague idea about their meanings. It can also be irritating when someone insists on using sophisticated vocabulary as a means of gaining advantage over you. Such people have failed to grasp the fundamental principle of effective verbal communication that we established earlier; namely, to remember your listener and aim for a shared understanding.

It is important to take care over the vocabulary we use. Experienced teachers can become so familiar with their subject that they use terms and expressions without regard to the fact that the listeners do not have a shared understanding of them. Acronyms litter the talk, conceptually difficult phrases are introduced without explanation as to their meaning, reference is made to several inter-related terms, and the listeners struggle to understand what is meant.

It is also important to be aware that language usage changes over time. Consider the following line from the original version of a well known children's hymn: 'There is a green hill far away <u>without</u> a city wall...' and the marked contrast with a more recent version of the same song: 'There is a green hill far away <u>outside</u> a city wall...'.

The older rendering made sense when it was written during the nineteenth century as the word 'without' was the considered to be the opposite of 'within'. However, the word 'without' now means 'did not possess', as in the expression 'She went without her gloves'. What the hymn writer meant to say was that the green hill was outside the city wall and not, as the old meaning implies, that the green hill did not have a city wall of its own!

Younger children, in particular, may not grasp a word or re-interpret it to fit their own experience. For instance, the little child who reformulated the line of the Lord's Prayer 'Lead us not into temptation' into 'Lead us not into Thames Station'.

The moral of the tale is clear: we must take care about what we say, not only because our words might get in a tangle or sound absurd, but innocent expressions from yesteryear can take on wholly different meanings with today's youngsters.

Activity 16

1. Record part of a lesson in which you do a lot of speaking. Listen to the recording and note any words which may have been confusing or ambiguous.

2. Following the lesson, ask two or three trustworthy pupils about any words or terms that you used during a lesson that they found confusing or peculiar.

Finally, even the most experienced people can get themselves in a tangle over words by using ambiguous phrases. The following three examples, taken from newspaper headlines, illustrate the point:

a) After a British man was held in Turkey until the New Year over alleged possession of drugs – **'British man kept in Turkey over Christmas'**.

b) After a commanding officer flew back to the front line to take charge of operations – **'General goes back to front'**.

c) After an unexploded bomb was found at the seaside – **'Shell found on beach'**.

Mishearing words

Word confusion is not confined to young children. Adults will often think that they understand what someone is saying, only to exclaim a few moments later: 'Oh, I thought you said (a different word from the actual one, though similar in sound)..!' causing considerable mirth in some cases. The likelihood of wrongly hearing what is said is increased under certain conditions:

- When there is a lot of background noise, in which case it is necessary to speak more slowly and distinctly.
- When the speaker talks too quickly or introduces ideas too rapidly, the solution for which is obvious.
- When the listener is still engaged with a previous conversation or preoccupied with a different agenda.

Your listeners' inability to understand what you are saying may have more to do with one of the above three factors than with the quality of your utterances.

Conclusion

In addition to making the best use of our natural voices, we must also consider a number of organisational and lesson management factors if we are to facilitate effective verbal communication. The most attractive voice in the world will be wasted if other factors are not taken into consideration. The following points can be used as a checklist:

- thorough preparation;
- thinking through in advance the words we intend to use and the way in which we use them;
- putting our listeners at their ease as quickly as possible;
- knowing the purpose or intentions we hope to achieve through what we say;
- engaging the audience by our enthusiasm and appropriate approach to the task in hand;
- getting the correct pitch and speed;
- pacing our speaking without becoming laborious;
- saying enough but not too much;
- using appropriate non-verbal signals;
- correct positioning in the room;
- using visual aids;
- varying our speech forms.

Developing effective communication skills allows us to impart information, offer helpful exemplars, create a thinking climate amongst our audience and, at best, cause people to change the way they live, think, feel and respond. They can help us to inspire, stimulate and encourage others. Make them a top priority.

Chapter 3

Speaking and listening

Listen; do you want to know a secret? Do you promise not to tell?
Closer; let me whisper in your ear; say the words you long to hear.
(Lennon and McCartney, Do You Want to Know a Secret)

It is difficult to identify specific factors which relate to each aspect of teacher-pupil communication, as different audiences and purposes require different approaches. Nevertheless, the task of teachers at all levels of schooling or training is to present information and stimulate thought in a systematic, comprehensible form, using language which allows pupils to understand and interpret their words, and imaginative strategies to support the learning process.

Speaking and listening in classrooms

The introduction of the National Curriculum re-kindled interest in the importance of speaking and listening in learning, by stressing the need for teachers to give pupils opportunities to talk for a range of purposes, to listen carefully and with understanding to what others say and to communicate in a clear, fluent and interesting manner (DfE, 1995). Older pupils were to contribute to arguments, communicate complex meanings and question carefully the things that others said. The classroom environment is to become a place where speaking and listening is central to learning. The teacher's task is to facilitate opportunities for pupils to extend their communicative competence and provide the circumstances for it to take place (see Chapter 5).

Quotations from English in the National Curriculum (DfE, 1995)
Pupils should be encouraged to speak with confidence, making themselves clear through organising what they say and choosing words with precision. (Section 2a, KS 1)

Pupils should be given opportunities to consider their own speech and how they communicate with others. (Section 3a, KS 1)

In discussions, pupils should be given opportunities to make a range of contributions, depending on the activity and purpose of the talk. (Section 2a, KS 2)

They should be taught to listen to others, questioning them to clarify what they mean, and extending and following up the ideas. (Section 2b, KS 2)

Pupils should be encouraged to develop both their communicative skills and their ability to evaluate language use. (Section 1d, KS 3/4)

In taking different roles in group discussions, pupils should be introduced to ways of negotiating consensus or agreeing to differ. (Section 2a, KS 3/4)

Teachers have to consider their own role in modelling good verbal behaviour and encouraging pupils to contribute effectively. In doing so, they have to recognise that at least five factors influence the nature of the speaking and listening that takes place in classrooms:

- The age of the pupils;
- Their previous experience of verbal interactions;
- A healthy classroom environment;

- The size of the group;
- The organisation for learning.

Age of pupils

The age of pupils is bound to make a difference to the nature of pupil-teacher and pupil-pupil communication. Four year-old entrants to school will not, of course, possess the same vocabulary, experience of adults, social awareness and conversational skills as older pupils. On the other hand, age itself cannot be used as an absolute guide to the communication level, as pupils of similar age may vary considerably in their ability to speak, listen and respond, depending upon their life experiences, personality and confidence. Even older pupils may not possess sophisticated listening skills and will be selective about the things they choose to hear.

It is important that teachers take account of the age phase in their use of language and vocabulary, and do not make assumptions about pupils' understanding of key words and expressions. The use of analogy and parable also has to be used with care, as it is only when pupils reach Key Stage 2 (seven years plus) that they begin to discriminate between reality and fantasy. Age is less significant than the inexperience of the pupils concerned, their maturity level, and the influence of speaking-and-listening in the home environment.

Previous experiences

Pupils may or may not come from a background in which verbal communication has been facilitated. Many factors can influence the quality of pupils' ability to communicate, including the dominance of television in the household, the lack of responsiveness between family members, the position of the individual in the hierarchy and the effect of humiliating or unsatisfactory verbal encounters at home or school.

Many experienced teachers will testify about occasions when they have been met by looks of incredulity by parents when describing their children's passivity in the classroom. Can this really be the same noisy, talkative child that lives at home! Nevertheless, communication skills cannot be assumed. When meeting a new class for the first time, wise teachers invest time and effort in developing a programme of study which will allow pupils to acquire the necessary skills for making a substantial contribution to class discussion.

Classroom environment

Pupils speak to teachers they can trust, and are prepared to listen to teachers they respect. Teachers can enhance the strength of their relationship with pupils and provide the climate for easier communication by means of the following:

Genuinely valuing pupils' verbal participation

This can be achieved through warmly encouraging everyone to participate, giving recognition for contributions, demonstrating acceptance and openness to other's ideas, friendly and responsive to the group as a whole.

Keeping the atmosphere light but purposeful

This can be achieved by maintaining a relaxed voice tone, concentrating on the task and avoiding nagging or personal remarks. Once good class order is established, there is room for increased amounts of humour, occasional diversions from the main task and a willingness to share insights.

Establishing class norms for verbal transactions

By expressing expected standards and goals and gaining class agreement about group norms and procedures, class norms can be established.

Encouraging a spirit of harmony and compromise

This can be done by persuading pupils to think constructively about their differences in opinion by searching for common factors in resolving conflicts, and trying to reconcile disagreements through debate.

Teaching good listening skills

Set a good example by helping each pupil to really listen to others and understand what they are saying. Promote a questioning attitude and regularly summarise points.

Encouraging pupils to express their feelings

Ask pupils how they feel about the way in which the group is working and about each other, and encourage them to share their feelings openly.

Monitoring the quality of pupil interactions

Observe the process by which the group is working and use those observations to monitor the quality of group cohesion.

(Further discussion about teacher-pupil relationships can be found in Chapter 4.)

Activity 17

1. How do you rate yourself on the seven factors noted above, using the categories:
Strong/Satisfactory/Weak.
2. Using the descriptors under each item concentrate on improving the weaker elements over the next week.
3. Using the three categories (Strong/Satisfactory/Weak), re-evaluate your skill levels at the end of the time period.
4. Select those factors that are still unsatisfactory and repeat the process until you are satisfied with the standard.

Larger groups

Larger group sizes influence the extent and quality of teacher-pupil communication in four ways:

- The teacher has to address a larger number of individuals, each with his or her own perceptions, intellect and experience of the subject.
- Larger numbers mean that there is statistically less opportunity for an individual pupil to make a verbal contribution.

- Larger groups limit many pupils' willingness to contribute.
- The larger the group, the harder the teacher may have to work to produce an intimate atmosphere.

On the other hand, a large group offers anxious individuals some anonymity and reduces the chances of them being chosen to speak by the teacher. Pupils can, if they wish, remain relatively anonymous (Pye, 1987).

Activity 18

1. Make a list of those pupils who keep a low profile in class.

2. Construct opportunities for them to make verbal contributions in smaller groups by placing them with less assertive pupils and giving them a specific task to do, such as

- allocating roles within the group
- reporting back
- summarising on behalf of the group.

3. Make sure that the pupils' contributions are quietly, but publicly acknowledged.

4. Take an opportunity to thank them personally for their contributions.

Avoid being gushingly enthusiastic about their enhanced role, but ensure that they efforts are recognised.

Organisation for learning

Teachers organise for learning in a variety of ways (see also Chapter 5). Some teachers will spend most of their time directly addressing the whole class, while others divide pupils into groups at the earliest opportunity and allocate tasks for the groups.

Teachers who work with the whole class at the same time may choose to use:

- a **transmission** approach; that is, the teacher talks and the pupils listen;
- a **reciprocal** approach in which they initiate the talk but invite pupils to contribute by use of questions or comments;

■ an **interactive** approach in which there is a free flow of ideas and opinions operating within an agreed framework of conduct.

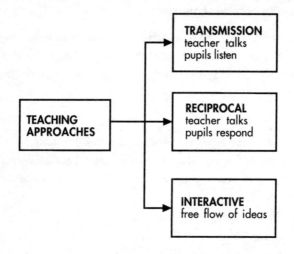

Figure 6 – Working with the whole class at one time

Organising for learning in which reciprocal or interactive teaching predominates allows for pupils to receive immediate verbal feedback from the teacher . However, teachers may find themselves commenting on what the pupil says rather than accepting the response as it stands. If teachers make too many approving or disapproving comments about the acceptability of the response, there may be a tendency for pupils to withhold an answer or idea for fear of public rebuke or humiliation, and the benefits of interaction are lost.

Teachers who favour group work are able to circulate around tables, offering advice, intervening where necessary and encouraging or praising pupils for their individual or combined efforts. However, the composition of groups is a key factor in facilitating good quality verbal interaction (see Chapter 5).

Organising for learning in which group work predominates allows for more verbal communication but limits the extent to which the whole class becomes aware of the teacher's advice, the existence of good practice and the verbal contributions made by pupils from a different group, unless the teacher makes a point of regularly announcing significant happenings and findings to the whole class.

1. Teachers should value pupils' answers more and make fewer qualifying remarks until after the responses are complete. Incorrect or unsubstantial responses should be used to assist understanding, not to undermine pupil confidence.

2. Helpful verbal communication between the teacher and members of a group should be vocalised for the whole class whenever possible.

Activity 19

1. Decide the proportion of time you <u>intend</u> to devote to direct teaching and group work during two class-based lessons. For instance, 25% direct; 75% group.

2. After the lessons, reflect upon the time you <u>actually</u> spent. Compare and contrast the intended and actual.

The teacher's role

Delamont (1976) makes two important points about the teacher's role in classroom talk:

Teacher talk that pupils actually hear is mostly about issues of control, order and organisation, and less often about learning

'The teacher's strategy is firstly to make her expectations for the classroom explicit, and to state and re-state them frequently'. In this way, talk is perceived by pupils as a control device rather than a means of learning.

The response of pupils to the teachers' use of voice is 'to find out what the teacher wants and give it to her, as long as they can see some pay-off for themselves in terms of...peace and quiet'.

Teachers are sometimes slow to pick up pupil ideas and expand them or develop them within hearing of the whole class

It is frequently the case that in busy classroom situations, with many learners and only one teacher, purposeful communication is never going to be easily attained due to a variety of constraints:

DIFFERING EXPECTATIONS

LEARNING OUTCOMES

TIME CONSTRAINTS

MULTIPLICITY OF DEMANDS

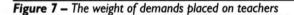

Figure 7 – The weight of demands placed on teachers

The physical, psychological and emotional demands made upon one teacher: with so many learners to deal with, teachers have to pace themselves and ensure that the frequency of verbal interactions do not leave them exhausted. It may be necessary to limit the range and extent of them.

The time constraints operating across a single lesson or session: although it is often desirable to spend more time in talk, the practicalities of deadlines, timetables and curriculum all conspire to reduce the options.

The pressure on the teacher to achieve particular learning outcomes with the pupils: lessons are rarely free from the need to reach specified outcomes or purposes. As talk is often targeted on learning outcomes, teachers have to restrict the number of verbal pathways, however fruitful, or risk being diverted too far from the main lesson purpose.

The teacher's and learners' expectations about the purpose of talk may be at variance: teachers may perceive verbal interaction as useful to achieve a desired outcome; learners may perceive it as a means of avoiding more onerous, less interesting forms of work.

Activity 20

While you might be pleased that pupils have engaged in meaningful speaking and listening, they are quite likely to go home and tell their parents that all they did during the lesson was talk! Justify to parents your use of pupils' talk in the classroom by writing comments under three headings:

- How it enhances pupils' **learning capability**.
- How it improves pupils' **social skills**.
- How it extends pupils' **thinking**.

Listening to pupils

Under the constraints described above, it is not surprising that teachers sometimes fail to utilise their communication skills effectively. In the busyness of classroom life, it is possible to receive pupils' comments at a superficial level and fail to hear what they are really saying. A pupil may be making an important point about a serious issue which is lost in the intensity of the moment. The teacher may be unaware of the real purpose of the comment or simply be too busy to give it adequate attention. In short, the teacher hears what is said but fails to listen to the thinking behind the words.

The ability to listen to pupils is, therefore, an essential communication skill and is deserving of serious study. Bolton (1979) points out that although we spend a large portion of our waking hours listening to people, broadcasts, music and the like, few of us are good listeners. He suggests that good listening needs to attend to three factors:

- **Attending behaviour** in which we show by our open body position and eye contact that we are interested in what is being said.
- **Following behaviour** in which we show by our silent attention, gentle encouragement and prompts that give speakers supportive space to explore their thoughts and ideas.

■ **Reflecting behaviour** in which we echo key words from what speakers say and try to summarise briefly what we believe they are saying as a means of empathising with their feelings.

Brown and Wragg (1993) propose four types of listening:

■ Skim listening when answers are relatively unimportant;

■ Survey listening in which you try to pinpoint the essence of what the pupil is saying;

■ Search listening in which you try to identify specific pupil answers;

■ Study listening in which you look beyond the pupil's words to the heart of what is really being said.

Nelson-Jones (1986) argues that listening 'is one of the most powerful psychological rewards that you can give', and that never being listened to is like a psychological death penalty. Rodenburg (1992) argues that the voices of males and females are naturally different and that women will 'question more, listen more attentively, make supportive caring noises and use a greater variety of inflection' whereas, by contrast, men 'tend not to listen so obviously, interrupt more frequently, dispute and interject, make dismissive noises or silently pretend not to hear what is being said'. She also claims that women tend to be supportive with their voices whereas men tend to dominate.

Activity 21

1. Select a series of lesson during which you make a conscious decision to listen more carefully to pupils' comments and demonstrate that you are doing so through your open body language, affirmative comments and genuine questions.

2. Reflect upon any differences that you notice compared with the normal level of engagement in terms of:

■ pupils' reactions;

■ the level of verbal interaction;

■ the rate of pupil's endeavours.

Nelson-Jones (1986) argues that good listening depends upon an ability to see things from the speaker's viewpoint rather than from your own.

Despite personal feelings (including dislike of the individual or a lack of respect for what the person is saying) a listener must allow speakers to say what they need to say and try to include a summary their feelings within the reply. The quality of our listening behaviour affects the willingness of pupils to offer their verbal contributions, in the knowledge that they will be genuinely considered and incorporated into the verbal interaction as a meaningful part of the deliberation.

The opportunity to model good listening skills relies to a large extent upon our ability to establish and control the classroom situation so that energy is spent on enhancing speaking and listening as a whole rather than repeating instructions, reinforcing procedural norms or exercising discipline.

Gaining and maintaining attention

It is important to gain the listener's attention before starting to speak, but as every teacher knows, it can be a major challenge with pupils or young people of any age (Bryson, 1998). There is little point in having something splendid to say if no-one is listening. We shall be examining strategies to assist class control in Chapter 6; suffice it to say for now that we cannot assume that our audience will want to hear our pearls of wisdom; we have to earn the right to be heard. Hitchman (1977) suggests that under normal conditions there are at least five points at which the intended message may not be adequately communicated. A modified version of Hitchman's points is listed in the table on page 56.

Table 3

Reasons for inadequate communication (after Hitchman, 1977)

1. Speakers may be unclear about what they want to say.

2. Speakers may have poor language skills and be unable to verbalise their thoughts.

3. Speech may be weakly articulated due to casualness, strong dialect or pupils' unfamiliarity with the teacher's speech patterns.

4. There may be intrusive noise.

5. The listener may not be paying attention because of:

■ *more interesting distractions;*

■ *psychological distress caused by what is being said;*

■ *verbal overload;*

■ *fatigue.*

These points are significant for teachers as they attempt to communicate with pupils. Neglect of some or all of them can interfere with effective communication of ideas. Horner (1970) writes:

> *...a lecturer might begin a lecture assuming that his students are sufficiently prepared, anxious to benefit from what they hear and intelligent enough to do so... Noticing poor response to the mere delivery of well-attested information, he attempts to evoke better response by strengthening his emphasis, by displaying personal conviction or by other non-intellectual means.*

Other **non-intellectual means** include sincerity, enthusiasm and sheer weight of conviction about the subject matter. Thus, 'earning the right' to teach will take time and perseverance, and will be determined by the extent to which:

■ the pupils believe that the lesson content is significant;

■ the teacher's voice is clear, interesting and understandable;

■ the teacher effectively uses different speech forms (such as describing, explanation, question-and-answer).

In the <u>earliest</u> stages of a lesson or when the whole class needs to be aware of something important, teachers need to use a variety of strategies to gain pupils' attention. Some teachers seem to believe that insisting that 'all eyes are on me' or 'let me have your full attention, please' will, of itself, ensure that pupils are ready and alert to listen to what is said. Although this call to order approach may have a reasonable chance of making sure that pupils hear what is said, it cannot guarantee that they are listening.

Activity 22

1. Assess your 'gaining and maintaining' strategies against Hitchman's five criteria noted above.

2. Ask a range of colleagues what strategies they use to engage a class's attention. List their answers.

3. Assess the usefulness of their ideas using the Hitchman criteria.

4. Gradually introduce suitable strategies into your own teaching and monitor the impact over a period of a few weeks.

It is difficult for teachers to ensure that pupils are properly engaged with their verbal commentary. After all, glazed eyes are not always distinguishable from captivated ones! However, basic requirements to maximise concentration include the following:

The teacher must be aware of what pupils already know and understand

There is little point in attempting to build on previous knowledge and conceptual certainty if pupils' grasp of these things is insecure. Unfortunately, it is easier to state this issue than to address it. After all, even if the group in front of us is only a dozen strong, it is not often practical to find out about each individual in detail.

Furthermore, even if it were possible to discover something meaningful about each pupil's knowledge and understanding, it may not be possible to spend the time addressing the problems that such insights expose. Some of them may be deeply rooted; others may be minor misunderstandings that can be quickly rectified. Either way, time has to be allocated to this essential task at the start of each session and during the session as appropriate.

The teacher must have something worth listening to

This point has been made elsewhere in this book, but it is worth underlining it. If we cannot convey the message to pupils through our voice tone, relevance and enthusiasm that the lesson content relates to their needs, it is hardly surprising if we lose their attention. It is also important to say that once the main verbal communication is at an end, our ability to provide interesting and well resourced activities will provide the bedrock for future good quality discussions.

The teacher must be able to intervene appropriately

Pupils require support as they work through their tasks and engage with the activities that are designed to enhance their understanding, increase their knowledge or improve their skill level. Intervention should not be so immediate that it detracts pupils from using their own initiative, or so slow that it makes them lose heart. The planned inclusion of deliberate interventions for the whole class to point out something noteworthy or re-direct their efforts is preferable to sudden loud comments which pupils are not sure whether to ignore or not. It is better to stop the whole class and specifically ask for their attention rather than making a general announcement to no-one in particular.

Hearing words spoken by a teacher (or anybody else) is not the same as listening. Listening is an active, conscious affair in which the receiver is tuned into the speaker's intentions and speakers are aware of, and taking into account, the impression created by their words.

Word pictures

If we talk to someone over the telephone, we may find ourselves using non-verbal signals, despite the fact that the other person cannot observe our actions. Instead, they listen for particular intonations in our speech patterns, the speed of our words, pauses between statements, and deviations from familiar interaction patterns to interpret our words. A mother may comment to her daughter that she sounds tired or enthusiastic or happy. A husband may ask his wife whether everything is alright or if she is upset about something. A person may gently ask a friend whether he has something else to tell him. Each of these reactions may be triggered by clues which arise less from the actual words that are spoken than the tone and emphasis placed upon them by the speaker:

- The mother may detect a slight slurring in her daughter's speech which suggests fatigue.
- The husband may note that his wife is more curt than normal and suspect that she is upset.
- The friend may become aware that the person he knows well seems to hesitate before speaking as though there were more to say.

Painting word pictures is an important part of verbal communication

If the speaker cannot be seen, the use of the sort of strategies outlined above are essential if the verbal interaction is to be meaningful.

Teachers in classroom situations are in the business of painting word pictures, normally supported by a variety of visual aids and other resources. The skilful use of descriptive phrases, challenging ideas and attractive possibilities, will stimulate and encourage pupils to engage with the task in hand. It is not always possible to provide the exciting lessons that stimulate and captivate our pupils, but we can at least ensure that our way with words creates the right verbal canvas on which to paint our learning objectives.

Conceptual development and explanations

We may consider it to be a reasonable claim that providing we use appropriate vocabulary, anything can be explained to any child of any age. Consider what form of explanation would be appropriate for a five year-old and a sixteen year-old in dealing with the topics listed below.

- What constitutes a healthy diet.
- What happens when water turns to ice.
- Why the tide moves up and down the beach.
- Why leaves fall off the trees.
- How gloves keep your hands warm.
- How bar codes work.

Note that the issues are grouped under three headings: **What? Why? How?**

- The 'What?' issues can be dealt with using factual information, such as the effect of different foods upon the body or the increase in volume when ice is formed.
- The 'Why?' issues require a deeper understanding of cause and consequence, and exceptions to the general rule, such as the impact of the land formation on tide movements or the differences between the leaf behaviour of deciduous and evergreen trees.
- The 'How?' issues demand that the teacher has a firm grasp of the scientific principles that lie at the heart of the process.

It is in the last of these explanations that the quality of teachers' verbal communication is tested; for whereas the 'what?' and 'why?' require a factual or considered response, the 'how?' involves the most explicit use of vocabulary and terminology. Words and phrases which would be adequate to satisfy the curiosity of a young child would hardly satisfy an examination candidate.

Effective explanations must take account of the purposes which are being served

Whereas a six year-old might be satisfied to know that woolly gloves keep the cold out and the warm in, a sixteen year-old science student would want to know how the body's physiology and heat transfer factors affect the overall temperature. A question about how bar codes work may require a detailed explanation about advanced physics or offer a general idea about the process using phrases such as 'recognises the product' or 'passes a signal to the machine' or 'tells the machine how much to charge'. While these explanations are correct, they do not convey anything which will allow the questioner to gain insights into the process which facilitate interpretation, analysis or an evaluation of the system.

The skilful communicator uses appropriate vocabulary

That is, vocabulary that is conceptually appropriate and suitable for the purpose. When six year-old Sadie asks her teacher 'where did you come from?' it is worth finding out whether she is interested in cities of birth or human reproduction! The most carefully presented explanations are wasted if the interpretation of the pupil's question is inadequate in the first place. It is important that teachers spend some time in clarifying what lies behind the question before an attempt is made to respond with the correct vocabulary.

Other explanations engage with moral issues

For example:

- why kittens die;
- what is true and what is false about a situation.

In these cases, terminology and understanding becomes more critical. Opportunities for pupils to respond with their own questions, and to gain reassurance about issues, must be made as accessible as possible within the constraints of a lesson. Moral issues require trust between pupil and teacher, an unpressurised atmosphere and precise, yet honest answers. Even young pupils will not be satisfied with platitudes or answers that avoid the issue for long.

Tell it like it is, but be willing to admit to uncertainty.

Activity 23

1. Tape record yourself offering an explanation to pupils.

2. Note the vocabulary and expressions that you employ.

3. Evaluate how successful you have been to take into account the three factors mentioned above, using the scale:
SUCCESSFUL/ADEQUATE/UNSATISFACTORY:

- taking account of the purpose being served;
- using appropriate vocabulary;
- engaging with moral issues.

4. Adjust your future speech patterns accordingly.

Genuine speech

We have all had the experience of entering a situation where 'you could have cut the atmosphere with a knife'. Such unpleasant circumstances are often associated with the <u>way</u> in which words are spoken, rather than the words themselves.

To a five year-old, a grown-up means what a grown-up says

Most pupils trust our words if they detect from our demeanour that we are genuine, even if they do not like what they hear. Older pupils become more sceptical but quickly decide whether we are telling the truth or making sense, depending upon the way our words match our actions.

Genuine speech is associated with tone of voice

We have all encountered the 'smooth talker' in whose voice there is a trace of something indefinably unsafe. For teachers, there is a balance to be struck between candour and common courtesy. This is especially relevant to our relationships with pupils whom we find it hard to like. It is unacceptable professional practice to make plain our dislike for individual pupils even if we strongly disapprove of their actions. It is important to use assertive speech at such times as a means of maintaining respect rather than adopting a hostile attitude.

The proof of our words is in whether we have to eat them!

Mutual respect

Mutual respect between the speaker and listener is an essential factor in establishing and maintaining effective communication. If we respect the person speaking, we are more likely to listen intently, respond positively and use our own words and non-verbal behaviour to encourage and re-inforce the speaker's self-worth.

Pupils listen to teachers if they believe they have something worth saying

However enthusiastically we may speak, if pupils find that our words have little relevance, they will turn off their receivers within moments. We end up transmitting across space to deserted planets! Similarly, if we display a disdainful or supercilious attitude towards our pupils, we can hardly be surprised if they adopt a negative stance towards us.

Nelson-Jones (1986) suggests that there are seven types of body language which send positive signals about our interest in what others are saying, and these are set out in the table below.

Table 4

Positive forms of body language (after Nelson-Jones, 1986)

- *Physical availability: simply being available when needed.*
- *Open and relaxed body posture: turning both your face and body towards the speaker.*
- *Slight forward lean: but not so far that it looks odd or invades the individual's personal space.*
- *Positive use of gestures: particularly gentle head nodding.*
- *Appropriate facial expressions: responding to the tone and content of what they are saying.*
- *Sensitivity to physical distance and height: with heads at about the same level and positioned at a non-threatening but sufficiently close distance.*
- *Appropriate use of touch: as a means of showing concern or sharing joy, but never outside the speaker's zone of comfort.*

The <u>use of touch</u> is a sensitive area today. It is important for teachers to be clear about the school or college policy on touching, especially when the teacher and pupil are of opposite gender. Some schools operate a strict no-touch policy. More often, teachers are expected to use their common sense about touching and never act in a way which might be misconstrued by pupils.

Activity 24

1. Take note of the interaction you have with pupils when you use an open face body position (as opposed to a sideways position) and Nelson-Jones' seven affirmative body gestures when listening to them speak, using the following criteria:

- the extent to which pupils appear to listen;
- their eye contact with you;
- their verbal response;
- the enthusiasm with which they then engage with the task.

2. Persevere with the open approach until it becomes a natural characteristic of your interaction with pupils.

Case studies

It is important to recognise that noteworthy examples of good communication all start from the premise that it is the <u>listener's</u> priorities, feelings and expectations that need to be central to the process rather than giving speakers opportunities to demonstrate their verbal dexterity. Nevertheless, teachers need to use their opportunities effectively. Contrast the following start of term talks by three teachers; try to 'hear' the words in your mind. What tone might be appropriate? Which words might be stressed? What are the teachers really trying to say?

Case 1: The student teacher

The lecturer to her examination class: 'You are here to gain a qualification. I am paid to help you get one. With your determination and my expertise we can make sure that the job is done. Welcome aboard!'

The lecturer will probably stress the words 'you' and 'I' and 'we' to emphasise the dual responsibilities, reinforced by the use of words like 'determination' and 'expertise' to focus upon the characteristics contributing to ultimate success. She introduces the concept of 'getting the job done' and extends an invitation which, though possible to decline, suggests that only through corporate endeavour will the desired goal be achieved. She slightly elongates her pronunciation of the word 'sure' to embed the concept of a positive outcome in her listeners' minds. The statement is characterised in four ways: i) an economical use of words; ii) affirming the obvious; iii) openness and sincerity; iv) establishing a sense of partnership.

Case 2: The primary teacher

The primary school teacher to her new set of pupils: 'You may have done well in the past, or badly; you may have messed about or worked hard; you may have been clever at your work or not so clever. Well, whatever you may have done or been, I want to tell you that in my class everyone has a fair chance. If you need to make a fresh start, I will help you; if you need to carry on from where you left off last year, I will help you. If you decide to waste your time or others, you will find that I can be as tough as old boots. The choice is yours.'

And, after allowing a few moments for them to think about what she had said, invited them to respond.

We can imagine that the teacher will use a firm tone. She will convey the impression that she is fair minded but not willing to tolerate silliness. She will encompass a range of pupil attitudes, abilities and experiences within her comments. We can envisage the slow pace of her final sentence 'the choice is yours', as she scans the class, picks up the pupils' gazes and offers them an opportunity to establish their position.

To some extent, Case 2 is an example of using words to convey a number of important messages about seniority (the teacher makes the statement, not one of the pupils); about hierarchy (the teacher decides who will receive help and who will be dealt with toughly); and about ownership (the pupils are invited to respond rather than merely accept the statement at face value). The central issue is the form of words used by the teacher and the meaning they convey rather than whether or not such a statement is appropriate or approvable.

Case 3: The secondary teacher

More controversial, perhaps, was the teacher who used to begin the year by saying to the class: 'This room can be a classroom or a prisoner of war camp. Make up your minds which you prefer. Just remember that if you choose the latter, I will be the commandant!'

In this case, the teacher is using the powerful imagery of war in his statement. As in Case 2, the choice offered by the teacher is stark, but this time the words sound divisive, even threatening. We can imagine that the teacher's tone would be slightly fierce, his manner forbidding, his body language rigid. There would not be a genuine choice but instead a strong suggestion that any failure to respond appropriately would be dealt with severely. Only the brave or ignorant would be foolish enough to invite the self-imposition of a prison camp regime!

The three cases used above are intended to illustrate the way in which words convey meaning, both in their use and the way in which they are spoken. In a different context, the same words would give a different impression, depending on who the speaker was and who the listeners were. Imagine, for instance, the startled looks on the faces of the listeners if the words of Case 3 were used with undergraduate students or those of Case 2 were used with four year-old nursery children. Words convey meaning which will vary according to the circumstances and wise teachers will think hard about the impact that their words have upon those who receive them.

Chapter 4

Classroom talk

The skills of listening, explaining, questioning and responding are important in themselves as well as being crucial for the development of intellectual skills.

(Brown and Atkins, 1987)

Talking comes naturally to most people. When listening to students in the bar, young pupils in the kindergarten or teenagers after a school sports match, it becomes obvious that they can talk at length about issues that matter to them. Paradoxically, the same group in a classroom setting may be silent or limited in their willingness to converse. Constructive classroom talk cannot be assumed; it needs to be developed and encouraged by the teacher. In doing so, two key questions have to be addressed:

- What is 'constructive talk' and how can it be distinguished from 'unconstructive talk'?
- What strategies are available to promote effective verbal communication in classrooms?

In attempting to answer these questions in this chapter and in Chapter 5, we need to recognise that teachers are engaged in many verbal encounters which, despite the availability of sophisticated micro-technology, provides the life blood of teaching and learning.

Home and school

Fox (1995) notes that whereas pupils initiate a large number of conversations when at home, the incidence falls dramatically once they are at school. We might add that children also decide for themselves when they have had enough of talking about something while at home, whereas in school, it is the teacher who most often terminates the dialogue. Similarly, Tizzard and Hughes (1984) noted that children talked freely at home about a wide range of topics, initiating and sustaining conversations, and intellectually struggling with ideas. Their verbal behaviour at home was in marked contrast to that in school.

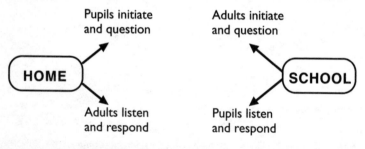

Figure 8 – *Patterns of verbal interaction at home and school*

Teachers normally control the dialogue and allow a restricted range of communicative options to the pupils, who rarely stray beyond the teacher's implicit agenda. Pupils who do so may be perceived as awkward or intrusive or threatening the teacher's control.

> By comparison with reading and writing, speaking and listening continues to be neglected in coverage, planning for progression, and assessment (QCA, 1997).

Shared understanding

Teachers talking does not ensure pupils are listening, and if they are listening, that they are understanding. For example, the teacher may be able to discuss issues dispassionately and objectively, whereas the pupils may still be at the stage of unthinking loyalty to a particular viewpoint.

Following their initial explanation about what the lesson comprises, teachers will sometimes ask their pupils if they understand. By asking this, the teacher may be referring to a number of different forms of understanding:

- **Procedural** – whether the pupils understand what they have to do.
- **Expository** – whether the pupils have grasped a principle or concept about which they were formerly unsure.
- **Regulatory** – when a class have to be reminded of the rules or conditions governing an activity.

Young pupils will often reply with a resounding 'yes' when asked if they understand, even when it is not altogether true, either because they are nervous about admitting their uncertainty in case they are ridiculed or because they have learned by experience that the teacher will not be satisfied until they do so. Older pupils and young adults are less likely to be as co-operative but may, if they are tired of hearing the teacher's voice or anxious to get on with the task in hand, verbally concede that they understand, while tacitly accepting among themselves that they prefer to make the best of a bad job rather than listen to further explanations (or recriminations). If the end of the session is approaching, the likelihood of older pupils admitting that they would like clarification from the teacher is remote, as any of their number raising an issue near the end of the lesson to gain favour with the teacher is likely to be very unpopular with peers if it holds up their departure!

Another more sophisticated way of expressing the question 'Do you understand?' might be: 'Do you share the meaning of the words I am using?' or perhaps: 'Is this making sense to you?' or again: 'Are my words making connections between us?'. The issue of shared meaning lies at the heart of effective verbal exchanges, as verbal communication can only be effective if words convey to the listener what was intended by the speaker. Classroom life can be awash with words, but unless what we say is making sense to our pupils, we may as well not bother.

Sometimes a small number of words can carry a lot of meaning

Consider the modern statement of faith: 'One person with God is a majority' or the Christian Aid slogan: 'We believe in life before death'. The power of these expressions is found in the way that they use familiar phrases with small but significant alterations to the wording, which cause us to stop and wonder whether we have heard or read it correctly.

Activity 25

1. Next time you have told the class about something, ask them if they understand what you have said. If they reply that they do, give them one minute to explain to the person sitting next to them.
2. Now ask the question: 'How many people were satisfied with the explanation they got from their partner?' and proceed accordingly.

Vocabulary

Teachers should be striving to enter the pupils' conceptual framework by using appropriate vocabulary and expressions. All too often it works the other way around as pupils attempt to gain understanding by interpreting the teacher's words and stay within the teacher's 'zone of satisfaction', by pretending to understand far more than they do. Pupils are aware of the danger of antagonising or frustrating their teachers, who may judge from their questions and comments that they are being awkward or 'not trying' rather than trying to get closer to the meaning. More experienced teachers will work hard to use pupils' vocabulary and familiar situations to enhance their explanation and interpretation. That is, the teacher will work from the pupils' understanding to assist them in gaining further insights.

It is not wise to assume anything about pupils' reception of the spoken word. For instance, a six year-old child who had seen his mother play This Little Piggy with his younger sister many times was surprised to hear that the 'wee-ee' sound was the sound of the excitement and not the noise of the frightened pig wetting itself! As teachers, we need to be careful not to convey wrong impressions, however unintentionally, that become so imprinted in pupils' minds that they hinder understanding.

The effect of classroom climate on talk

To establish a classroom setting in which there is good pupil-pupil and pupil-teacher communication, two key things have to be in place: first, the teacher needs to encourage pupils to talk to one another within limits agreed beforehand and for accepted purposes; second, pupils need to feel that there if they offer public verbal contributions, what they say will be accepted and valued without causing them humiliation or embarrassment. If verbal communication is to play a key role in learning, teachers and pupils have to be convinced that it is enhanced through opportunities for talking and listening.

It may take time before a classroom climate can be established in which verbal exchanges are acknowledged by pupils as making a significant contribution to learning. Some groups of pupils may have previously experienced a rigid form of classroom instruction, dominated by teacher talk, in which the extent of their verbal contribution has been confined to responding to teacher-led questions. Other pupils may have been encouraged to express their thoughts in a class discussion but rarely had opportunity to collaborate in smaller, secure group settings. Yet others may have had an excess of collaborative group discussions but been offered little chance to speak openly in whole class debates.

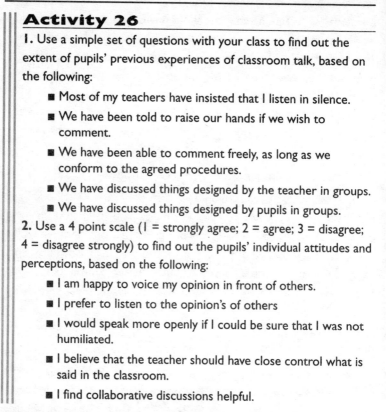

Activity 26

1. Use a simple set of questions with your class to find out the extent of pupils' previous experiences of classroom talk, based on the following:

- Most of my teachers have insisted that I listen in silence.
- We have been told to raise our hands if we wish to comment.
- We have been able to comment freely, as long as we conform to the agreed procedures.
- We have discussed things designed by the teacher in groups.
- We have discussed things designed by pupils in groups.

2. Use a 4 point scale (1 = strongly agree; 2 = agree; 3 = disagree; 4 = disagree strongly) to find out the pupils' individual attitudes and perceptions, based on the following:

- I am happy to voice my opinion in front of others.
- I prefer to listen to the opinion's of others
- I would speak more openly if I could be sure that I was not humiliated.
- I believe that the teacher should have close control what is said in the classroom.
- I find collaborative discussions helpful.

Contexts for pupil talk

Teachers who genuinely want to enhance the level of pupils' verbal contributions will need to be convinced that the talk will enhance rather than deplete learning and want to identify opportunities for doing. Dougill and Knott (1988) suggest that in a verbally rich classroom setting, pupils should have the opportunity to:

- ask relevant questions;
- tell a story;
- persuade someone;

- chat;
- speculate;
- think aloud;
- negotiate;
- give instructions;
- complain;
- argue (and win graciously);
- express or disguise feelings;
- reach judgements;
- summarise and arrive at a point of decision.

Teachers need to be clear about what they are trying to achieve with pupils

Some forms of talk occur naturally from day to day; others require managing if they are to have the maximum impact. For instance, it might be easier to involve pupils in story telling than in having to persuade others to their point of view, depending upon the age and maturity of the pupils and the circumstances of the lesson. Young children have a limited grasp of time and the relationship between different events; older pupils may be embarrassed about being in role whereas primary-aged pupils normally enjoy activities involving pretence. Teachers may want pupils to reach judgements or be left in a state of uncertainty about a complex issue until a future occasion. It is axiomatic that the nature of the verbal interaction must always link closely with lesson objectives and learning intentions.

Achievement is not measured solely in the quality of talking and learning that takes place but also in the measurable outcomes and evidence that learning has been secured. Some teachers may not feel that they can afford the luxury of pupils chatting about the work when deadlines have to be reached and examinations passed. The teacher who enthuses at a Parents' Evening about the quality of the child's verbal contributions and consequent growth in confidence, but has to admit to the child's relative academic failure, is unlikely to convince parents that the time has been well used! Nevertheless, the heart of effective verbal communication is that as teachers help pupils to develop and use their spoken language skills, the impact will be beneficial to motivation and learning.

Some things which require a straightforward response and understanding in one context can assume a wholly different meaning and generate different reactions in another (Silverstein, 1974). This is particularly true when we ask questions. An apparently simple question may be interpreted in several ways according to the context. For instance: 'Were you there last Friday?' is a question which does not carry any threat if casually asked by a friend who is simply interested in the latest gossip, but may be sinister if asked by a barrister in a court of law!

Edwards and Furlong (1978) explain the importance of situation as follows:

> Hearing an utterance which is not immediately intelligible, they refer to their knowledge of the situation to narrow the range of possible meanings... What is meant on that occasion may depend on who the speaker is, on when and where he is speaking, and on his relationship to the listener.

They argue that pupils will assign meaning to what teachers say, depending upon the quality of their relationship. If pupils are at ease with the teacher, they will accept teachers at their word, ask questions to clarify their understanding and spend little or no time worrying about subtle meanings and how the teachers' words should be interpreted. If the teacher-pupil relationship is uneasy, pupils may examine the teacher's words more carefully to detect hidden meaning and innuendo.

Teacher dominance in verbal exchanges

Because teachers tend to dominate classroom talk and pupils have to listen to what is said throughout the majority of lessons, teachers have to try and ensure that every pupil is tuned in to what they are saying; that is, that pupils are interested and can make sense of the flow of words. Barnes (1975) reminds us that pupils have to learn how to interpret what teachers say. Teachers, in turn, need to consider the extent to which their words might be interpreted literally and the stage of the pupils' language development. Pupils use language in their attempts to make sense of the world, so that 'learning to communicate is at the heart of education'.

In the average classroom, someone is talking for two-thirds of the time, two-thirds of that is teacher talk and two-thirds of that is direct influence (Flanders, 1970).

Once the parameters for involvement have been established, and pupil involvement has been invited and secured, teachers need to build in opportunities for responses in a way which enhances rather than detracts from the learning.

The teacher role is highly significant in controlling the balance of verbal exchanges in the classroom

A more passive teacher role assumes a more active one for pupils. If the teacher initiates and controls the interaction closely, the spontaneity of responses is limited by the extent to which the teacher allows individuals to express their opinion, offer suggestions or provide solutions without interruption. If the teacher chooses to step back and allow pupils to create patterns of verbal interaction, there is more chance that dominant pupils will become too assertive and milder pupils will elect to not take part at all. The worst scenario imaginable is for the teacher to relinquish authority in such a way that the interaction becomes a verbal slanging match. On the other hand, excessive teacher dominance can result in a suppression of pupil ideas or an inert atmosphere of sterile comment and predictable reactions. These extremes can be presented as follows:

EXCESSIVE TEACHER DOMINANCE leads to PUPIL PASSIVITY AND LOW LEVEL INTERACTION
EXCESSIVE PUPIL DOMINANCE leads to LOSS OF TEACHER CONTROL

If classroom talk is to produce worthwhile outcomes, we should consider that teachers and pupils both have something to contribute. These contributions will be enhanced if teachers are prepared to ease their grip on their traditional role of dominating the talk.

Activity 27

(1) Rank yourself on a scale from 1 (strongly) to 5 (weakly) in terms of the pupils' passivity in most of your lessons. Is this because you believe that they learn best in this way or because you are concerned about control factors?

(2) Write down three improvements that you would you ideally like to see in terms of pupils' verbal contributions.

Teachers' concerns about pupil involvement

Not all teachers are keen to extend opportunities for classroom talk. Teachers' resistance to inviting pupil contributions can take many forms.

- Those who are afraid to allow pupils too much opportunity, lest they take advantage of the opportunity and the lesson is spent restoring control rather than achieving anything worthwhile.

- Those who are concerned about time factors; they are aware of all that has to be covered and the importance of maintaining a particular rate of progress.

- Those who believe that unless they are doing most of the talking, they are not earning their money.

It must be acknowledged that a strategy for effective verbal communication in which pupils' are actively invited to contribute is not without its risks. Teachers have to decide whether the risks are worth the likely benefits to the learning process.

Partnership in learning is not the same as relinquishing responsibility; rather, it is about valuing the contribution made by each person in the group and emphasising the importance of the collaborative endeavour.

Creating a rich verbal ethos

There are two significant factors which constitute the bedrock of a verbally rich classroom in which speaking and listening forms an integral part of the learning process.

The teacher's relationship with pupils

Pupils are very observant and sensitive to teachers' moods, behaviour and preferences. Teachers who resort neither to sanctions nor hectoring, who do not jump to conclusions, who listen carefully to pupils' comments and who enthuse about the work, are more likely to be popular with pupils than those who are unresponsive, detached and self-opinionated. Pupils are also appreciative of teachers who are themselves interesting people.

Although the right classroom climate facilitates verbal interaction, it is also true that an essential component in creating a positive learning environment in the first place is the quality of the verbal communication. The two are inextricably linked. Wise teachers take care what they say and how they say it. They are not afraid of words but rather aware of how easily misunderstandings can arise and offence can be taken if inappropriate words are used. They know that the right word at the right moment can transform attitudes and open up new worlds of opportunity.

Most pupils need to be made to feel special, not because they are vain or inadequate, but because they are human. Nonetheless, it is not always easy to enthuse and inspire learners, and inexperienced teachers or those with troublesome pupils in the class will find it difficult to make substantial progress, regardless of their efforts (see Bryson, 1998, Chapter 3).

Pupils who seem impervious to a reasoned approach

The conduct and behaviour of such pupils invites, and sometimes needs to receive, a firm response. Some teachers find that the wearisome daily battles with small groups of pupils detracts from the pleasure of teaching and the establishment of a healthy verbal climate. Teachers hear their own voices getting louder and higher; they begin to interpret silliness as defiance, and counteract pupils' negative reactions with fierceness and an accusatory tone. Under testing circumstances, it is not surprising that teachers prefer to retain a tightly controlled, direct delivery style, as they feel that it offers them a greater chance of maintaining acceptable levels of behaviour than the more demanding interactive approach.

Regardless of the constraints of having to deal with recalcitrant youngsters, it is worth reinforcing the point that positive relationships with pupils is enhanced by knowing about them: their wants, their needs, their hopes and their fears. Such knowledge takes time to acquire and, in some cases, it is not possible to do the process justice due to insufficient opportunity, pupils' aloofness or social constraints (such as cultural factors). Nevertheless, an understanding of pupils' backgrounds and what motivates them can make a significant difference to the way in which we communicate our expectations about the quality of a particular pupil's responses.

Enjoying a good relationship with pupils should not be seen as a contrived friendship for friendship's sake, but as an important factor in the maintenance of good order and an effective working ethos (Woods, 1987), in which it is possible to enhance the quality of the teacher-pupil and pupil-pupil verbal interactions.

Activity 28

1. Note which one of the following most accurately describes your <u>intentions</u> as a teacher.

- Responsive and supportive at all times.
- Friendly but retaining a professional distance.
- Unpredictable.

2. Contrast your answer with the way you think your pupils
<u>perceive</u> you.

- You are responsive and supportive and enjoy an open
  healthy relationship with them. You speak courteously to
  them and insist on the same in return.
- You keep a certain distance from them and your speech is
  measured rather than warm. You offer them sufficient
  support and encouragement without becoming too involved.
- You vary in your relationship with them. You can be friendly
  or aloof, depending upon the circumstances. You quite enjoy
  keeping them guessing about your mood and degree of
  receptiveness.

Note any mismatch between 1 and 2 and consider the likely
reason using the following:

- none of the above statements are sufficiently accurate;
- you do not know what relationship you want;
- your relationship varies according to the particular set of
  pupils you teach;
- you want to have a particular relationship but feel certain
  that pupils do not perceive you in the way you intend.

3. Write down <u>three</u> specific ways in which you can close the gap
between intended and actual classroom practice by a) improving
your relationship with pupils; b) listening and valuing their verbal
contributions more carefully.

In establishing and maintaining good communication, it is important to
consider relational factors carefully. The classroom ethos is not
dictated by the colour of the walls or the condition of the furniture,
but about the mutual respect among those present and the motivation
that can be engendered by teachers who not only use words well but,
as much as possible, support their words through the quality of their
actions and the provision of interesting and relevant lessons.

The teacher's response to pupils' contributions

Establishing valuable patterns of verbal interaction in classrooms does not happen by chance. Teachers often have to take account of pupils' former experiences in which talk was outlawed or kept under tight control. Pupils may have tried to contribute in the past but been shouted down by their peers, ridiculed by a teacher or dismissed out of hand. Less assertive pupils may feel that the effort is simply not worthwhile.

Openness and sincerity are two sides of the same coin.

- **Openness** is expressed through the use of plain but courteous speaking, non-threatening body language (such as smiling) and good eye contact (not glaring).

- **Sincerity** is transmitted through an earnest tone, leaving the listeners under no illusions about the fact that the speaker means business and intends to approach matters reasonably and without prejudice.

It is the teacher's task to put speakers at their ease before they can be expected to talk with confidence. If the teacher is only 'half' listening or gets impatient with pupils' attempts to verbalise their thinking, sensitive pupils lose the incentive to project their voices and lapse into a few stuttering words that fail to convey what they intended. The embarrassed individual is unlikely to venture making another contribution for some time.

Teachers are more likely to establish and promote effective verbal communication if they convince pupils that they are interested in their individual welfare, modelled through:

- giving them the chance to speak;
- listening intently to what they say;
- acknowledging their feelings, beliefs and preferences;
- allowing time for them to disclose matters of significance;
- speaking and acting courteously towards them;
- responding openly but considerately to the points they raise;
- avoiding favouritism and unfairness;
- insisting on a high standard of mutual respect from pupils.

As many different types of verbal interaction take place in classrooms, each of them will vary in the way in which the teacher and pupils contribute. For instance, a question-and-answer session in which the teacher initiates all of the questions is different from a debate about a contentious issue in which a variety of value positions are involved. Whatever the main purpose of the lesson, if pupils are going to feel comfortable in offering verbal contributions, then teachers have to be careful to avoid adopting unhelpful strategies such as:

- **Talking too much.** Instead, they should be willing to listen for longer.
- **Showing preference for a viewpoint too soon.** Instead, they should allow pupils to express a variety of views and make their suggestions before offering support for one opinion.
- **Pressurising the talker** by cutting in, asking abrupt questions abruptly, expressing dissent too quickly or insisting that pupils justify their position. Instead, they should give speakers space to explore their ideas and struggle with the concepts and issues raised.
- **Summarising the pupil's position** before they have finished speaking to hurry the lesson along. Instead, pupils should be invited to think through what they want to say, reach their own conclusions and express them in their own way.
- **Humiliating, ridiculing or scorning.** Instead, what pupils say should be treated with respect.
- **Meeting anger with anger.** Instead, allowing pupils opportunity to express their frustrations and give vent to their feelings without allowing the situation to deteriorate.

In particular, pupils who have not been given a lot of opportunity to make verbal contributions should be allowed to do so gradually, encouraged by teachers who are genuinely interested in hearing what they have to say. The process of confidence building takes time, but unless we do so, assertive pupils will dominate the proceedings at the expense of the timid ones and verbal interaction of any meaningful kind will be limited to the few.

Speech is not only a tool which each of us can use in making sense of the world, but also a means of imposing our version of the world on others (Barnes, 1975, page 116).

There is a difference between a classroom climate that provides a secure environment for pupils to take risks in talking and one which is just an ill-informed talking shop.

Rules of engagement for pupil participation

It is not enough for teachers to give a general welcome to pupils for them to participate in classroom discussions; the rules of engagement have to be made explicit.

A stranger in the average classroom might be surprised by the dominance of teacher talk, the passivity of many pupils and the highly structured nature of the lessons. Our visitor might also puzzle over the unspoken conventions that seem to be understood by the majority of pupils, such as who speaks and when, how others contribute to the discussion, and the verbal signals that indicate a willingness (for instance) to give way, accept a supplementary point or acknowledge inaccuracy. The visitor will note how the teacher often acts as arbitrator and frequently initiates new lines of discussion, raises alternative options and encourages or suppresses particular opinions.

These procedures have not emerged without a good deal of clarification about acceptable norms which have been gained through teacher insistence, pupil-teacher negotiation and a sparring for position that characterises many social situations. Teachers and pupils have eventually to reach an understanding about what is appropriate. This process may take days and weeks before it is secure; in the meantime, teachers have to resist the temptation to give up hope and revert to a more authoritarian situation before the interactive conventions have been given time to 'bed in' to the fabric of classroom life.

Activity 29

1. Write down your rules of engagement for a particular classroom session.

2. During the next lesson, note how many infractions occur.

3. Remind your pupils of them at the commencement of the next interactive time and note whether the number of infractions decreases.

4. Continue reminding pupils regularly and monitor the impact upon their behaviour.

A checklist for classroom talk

Although talking comes naturally to most people, the limitations of classroom life can result in a reduction of opportunities for learning through effective communication. Use the following points as a checklist as you consider the range and extent of classroom talk in your lessons.

- Plan and prepare lessons in such a way as to encourage the pupils' interest and involvement.
- Prepare and use open-ended questions which involve pupils and elicit responses that enhance learning.
- Explain things clearly and vary your voice tone and modulation as appropriate to the circumstances and age of pupils.
- Show interest, enthusiasm and sensitivity in talking and listening to the pupils.
- Respond to difficulties in a constructive and effective manner.
- Select and comment helpfully on significant classroom events.
- Devise opportunities for pupils to explore, experiment and engage in purposeful play (for younger pupils).
- Use good eye contact and meaningful body language as you speak.

Chapter 5

Teaching and learning

The role of language in learning is vitally important. It is the tool which we use to interpret, communicate, work through and make sense of our experiences.

(Lloyd and Beard, 1995)

We noted in Chapter 4 that teachers like to control the ebb and flow of classroom talk by initiating most teacher-pupil and pupil-pupil verbal communication through establishing the ways in which learning takes place. It is teachers, not children, who most often decide what is discussed and where, how and when it happens.

Over a period of time, pupils gradually develop an understanding of what is acceptable to the teacher. The teacher also makes concessions and takes into account, to a lesser or greater extent, the pupils' preferences and ideas. Both pupils and the teacher draw upon previous verbal exchanges to define the boundaries for talk, rehearse earlier points and redefine issues. Some elements of earlier discourse are used in formulating fresh ideas and refining concepts. The best form of classroom talk relies upon the active involvement of teacher and pupils to raise awareness and generate understanding.

Because pupils are sensitive to what teachers say and believe, they may be reluctant to say anything which conflicts with opinions that teachers have expressed. This means that even in what appears to be open discussion, pupils are aware of the teacher's previous comments and reactions, and may adjust what they say accordingly. For instance, if a teacher has been dismissive of certain pupil suggestions or failed to react enthusiastically to an idea or explanation, these points do not go unnoticed by the rest of the class. Less confident pupils are inclined to remain silent until some of their bolder peers have cleared the track for them, by volunteering comments and eliciting responses from the teacher which offer signposts as to what is acceptable and what is not. Some pupils may be keen to express their opinion or ideas but decide to wait until the teacher's preferences have been exposed before venturing a comment. The insecure pupil's eventual contribution is likely to be framed in a way which more closely reflects the teacher's preferences than would have initially been the case. It is important for teachers to realise their own influence in the content of pupils' verbal contributions.

Strategies teachers use for incorporating talk into the learning process

Five considerations are relevant:

- The extent to which the lessons are dependent upon teacher-initiated talk.
- The opportunities for groups of pupils to undertake collaborative discussion.
- The amount of pre-discussion information that pupils are given.
- The opportunities given to pupils (especially the less confident ones) to offer a verbal contribution.
- The way in which our reactions affect the willingness of pupils to offer further comment.

Activity 30

1. During your planning for a full day's teaching (or equivalent), decide how strongly each of the five points mentioned above will apply to each lesson.

2. Over the same lessons, note the proportion of pupils who fall into the following categories:

- those who only speak to their immediate neighbour;
- those who make some contributions;
- those who make a significant contribution.

3. Reflect on the underlying reasons that pupils make little contribution:

- they are not given opportunity;
- they are quiet by nature;
- they are not interested;
- they are intimidated by their assertive peers;
- the way you structured the lesson.

In making appropriate decisions about the five points above it is useful to take account of established theories of learning.

Theories of learning and verbal interaction

A consideration of the three most familiar theories of learning help us to locate the value of verbal communication in the learning process (Pollard, 1997). The three broad theories are

- Behaviourist theory
- Constructivist theory
- Social constructivist theory

Behaviourist theory

A teaching approach which is underpinned by behaviourist theory may suit a direct teaching approach in front of larger numbers of pupils in which differentiation on the basis of ability is not particularly significant. Characteristics of behaviourist theory are listed in the table below.

Table 5

Behaviourist theory

1. We learn by building up associations between our experience, thought and behaviour.

2. Information is transmitted by the teacher in an orderly, well structured way.

3. The teacher exercises control over the verbal exchanges and learners are largely passive.

4. There is an emphasis on repetition and rote.

Under what circumstances is a behaviourist approach likely to be suitable for teaching and learning in the age phase that you teach?

Good and Brophy (1986) summarised twenty years of research in American schools by saying that, in general, pupils who spent most of their time being instructed by the teachers or working independently under teacher supervision, made greater gains than students who were expected to learn largely on their own. Frequent instruction by the teacher was important, especially important for the lowest ability students. Laslett and Smith (1984) suggested that teaching should follow a 'Cycle' in which the following procedure is used:

- Start with seat work, recapping work previously taught.
- Introduce new work through teacher talk or demonstration.
- Make sure pupils grasp the new ideas by question and answer session.
- Practise examples by working as a group and then individually.
- Look back by reviewing the new learning and linking it to previous skills and knowledge.
- End with a short relaxing activity on a topic of interest to pupils.

Activity 31

1. Use the Laslett and Smith Cycle as a basis for planning a lesson.
2. Evaluate the worth of the lesson using the following criteria:
    - the effectiveness of the recapping;

- the form of talk you used to introduce the new ideas (explanation, demonstration...);
- the responsiveness of pupils during the question-and-answer session;
- the pupils' grasp of the new ideas as they practised and consolidated them;
- the effectiveness of your attempts to link previous and present learning;
- the positive conclusion to the lesson.

3. Note which aspects of the Laslett and Smith Cycle were inappropriate or less than satisfactory for your lesson. Make appropriate modifications during succeeding lessons on the same topic.

4. On the basis of your experience of implementing the Cycle, draw up a list of those lessons which lend themselves to this approach and those which do not.

Constructivist theory

Piaget is the name most often associated with constructivist theory. He argued that people learn to adapt to their environment and gain understanding about the world by encounters with the environment. As children experience the world, they pass through a series of stages associated with their ability to think about the world in more cognitively complex ways. Characteristics of constructivist theory are listed in the table below.

Table 6

Constructivist theory

1. As thinking is an activity, pupils need time to think.

2. Pupils need to accommodate their existing thinking into new experiences so that they can construct a more accurate understanding of what is going on.

3. The construction of these stages follows a sequence, characterised by the type of thinking skills used at each stage.

The impact of constructivist theory in classrooms has been to emphasise the need for younger children to play, discover for themselves and carry out practical investigations. Pupils are encouraged to think hard and offer suggestions about the way their own learning might be organised. However, constructivist theorists like Piaget failed to emphasise 'the central role that language has to play in developing a child's understanding and the essential role of adults...' (Fisher, 1995).

To what extent has the constructivist approach been reflected in the classrooms in which you have worked as a teacher? What forms of talk have been evident?

Social constructivist theory

This theory strongly suggests the importance of the social context and interaction with others to enhance learning. Vygotsky and Bruner have been influential in developing this theory. Vygotsky argued that if pupils are offered appropriate support, they will progress beyond their current state to achieve their full capability. The 'gap' between the child's present and potential level of understanding is referred to as the Zone of Proximal Development, ZPD, (see Kerry, 1998, Chapter 1). The assistance in learning may come from the teacher or from another child or from within a group of children discussing together. Interaction with other pupils allows individuals to examine their ideas and beliefs and develop their thinking. As the intervention and support of others is likened to 'scaffold' placed around a house as it is constructed, the support received by a child across their ZPD is referred to as scaffolding. The scaffold is gradually removed as individuals gain confidence and reach their potential. The context in which the talk takes place is important as well as the tasks which are undertaken. Social constructivism has implications for classroom practice, as can be seen in the table on page 90.

Table 7

Social constructivist theory and classroom practice

- *Collaborative problem solving is recognised as a helpful strategy for sharing ideas and opinions.*
- *Drafts of written work are shared with other pupils allows for a critical dialogue which enhances the quality of the final product.*
- *Completed work is reviewed as a means of enhancing and extending pupils' shared experiences.*

The learning environment

The traditional learning environment is described by Bird (1990) as '... generally passive, directed and conditioning. For many it results in the development of learned helplessness, in which pupils convince themselves that they cannot proceed without support from others, even in cases where they are capable of doing so. Bird claims that a satisfactory learning environment has eight characteristics, as shown in the table below.

Table 8

A satisfactory learning environment (after Bird, 1990)

1. *learner centred;*
2. *risk taking;*
3. *mistake making;*
4. *opportunities to make choices;*
5. *high expectations and standards;*
6. *opportunities to learn with others;*
7. *opportunities to learn through experience;*
8. *happens both inside and outside school.*

These eight characteristics are examined below in the context of effective verbal communication issues.

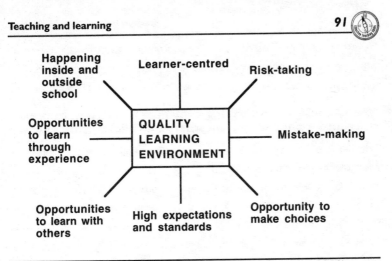

Figure 9 – Creating a quality learning environment (after Bird, 1990)

In a learner centred environment, the emphasis moves from teaching to the process of learning

As pupils are given more opportunity to take responsibility for their learning, they incorporate their own thinking into the learning process through sharing ideas, proposing solutions and trying different approaches. Teachers encourage pupil initiatives and are prepared to set their own preferences to one side to accommodate them.

We may be reluctant to be too accommodating of pupils' ideas because of our responsibilities to deliver a prescribed curriculum in a limited amount of time, with a decrease in opportunities for pupils to develop their communicative competence.

The level of verbal exchange increases significantly when pupils are actively encouraged to experiment and take risks

Pupils try things out and learn from what they are doing. Collaborative ventures in which the outcome depends upon the co-operation and combined expertise of the members of the group can enhance the pupils' use of language and lead to more varied and interesting outcomes than if individuals were to pursue the same objectives.

Nevertheless, there has to be a careful attention given to the extent to which the lesson objectives established by the teacher are affected by the freedom offered to pupils to show initiative and take risks in learning.

When pupils' fear of making a mistake is reduced, they can relax into a purposeful, unconstrained exploration of ideas

The heart of this approach is to encourage pupils to learn from their mistakes rather than worry about making them in the first place. Mistakes are viewed as opportunities for discussion about the source of the problem and reinforcement the principles underpinning the work. Mistake making is likely to be more relevant when the task involves problem solving or investigation. Teachers have to be careful not to allow mistaken ideas to settle in pupils' minds. There is a need to differentiate between <u>wrong</u> ideas and <u>elementary</u> ideas: wrong ideas require correcting; elementary ideas form the basis for further instruction and exploration of concepts.

We have to consider how long we allow pupils to make mistakes before offering the correct answer or interpretation. Early intervention may not allow pupils to discover their own errors; delayed intervention might reinforce wrong ideas in their minds.

Teachers have a responsibility to model the standards that they expect from their pupils

Teachers who are positive and optimistic in their approach with pupils, encourage them to set high standards for themselves, and put success and failure into perspective, are likely to develop a good learning environment with purposeful verbal communication.

Pupils are placed in groups to develop skills of interaction, communication and conflict resolution

We noted above the importance of pupils learning together and the potential benefits from tasks which not only required co-operation but a corporate sense of mutual purpose in which all members' expertise is necessary for a successful outcome. Teachers cannot assume that the skills which are needed for collaborative ventures will occur naturally.

Part of the teacher's job is to help pupils develop the skills for making the best of their opportunities, such as allocating responsibilities within the group, turn-taking, establishing social conventions for offering opinions, evaluating ideas objectively, assertiveness, drawing conclusions, representing and presenting findings. Inexperienced teachers may become discouraged when collaborative ventures do not result in immediate benefits. Perseverance and a clear action plan is essential.

Learning through experience is often equated with open-ended opportunities

Pupils are encouraged to encounter situations directly rather than being told about them, to be active in their learning, contributing ideas, offering suggestions, and generally making sense of things for themselves. However, learning through experience cannot be assumed. Many people never seem to learn, despite numerous ordeals and hard experiences! It is the teacher's task to encourage the conditions for learning in which experience offers the greatest benefits for pupils. One of the criticisms of this form of learning is that it involves too much time ineffectively used and casual verbal exchanges which do little to assist the learning process.

The ideal classroom environment is one in which pupils feel comfortable about voicing their opinions, asking questions, clarifying ideas, and revising concepts through oral, written and visual expression.

Clarifying the learning process for pupils

One important aspect of verbal communication is in clarifying for pupils the nature of the task, the reason for doing it and the expectations about the quality of the outcomes. In short, to let pupils know what is going on. Teachers need to spend some time at the start of each session reminding pupils of past discussions, summarising main points (or asking them to do so) before moving forward into the next stage of learning.

It is useful for teachers to put themselves in the pupils' place and ask the sort of questions that they might be asking. Proctor *et al* (1995) suggest eight such questions (see the table below).

Table 9

Questions pupils ask (after Proctor *et al*, 1995)

1. What am I doing?
2. Why am I doing it?
3. How am I supposed to tackle it?
4. Who will be doing this with me?
5. Where shall I do the task?
6. What things will I need in order to get on?
7. When should I have accomplished something?
8. What will happen to the outcomes?

The following comments relate to these questions.

Pupils need to know what they are doing and what the teacher expects from them

The older they get, the more pupils will benefit from being involved in the process of organising their own learning. Whereas very young pupils usually place complete trust in adults to tell them what to do, their helplessness is gradually replaced by a more discerning attitude about the task on which they are engaged. Teachers first have the responsibility to be clear themselves about what they expect from the pupils; otherwise, transmitting the necessary information will become unsatisfactory and pupils will receive the impression (correctly) that the teachers do not know what they are doing.

Pupils need to be told what is going on and to be informed about why it is happening

To give pupils a task to do without any indication about why it is necessary or an explanation about where it is leading, is to deprive them of a sense of ownership which exacerbates the separation of teaching from learning rather than enhances the feeling of being part of a single enterprise. Explanations about why an activity is being undertaken enable pupils to see the links between phases of learning. This is different from occasions in which teachers deliberately inject a sense of mystery and suspense into a situation to promote pupils' interest in genuinely investigative activities. There may also be times when a task has to be carried out because it is a required part of the programme, such as doing external tests or completing forms. Even when teachers are unconvinced about the value of what has to be done, they still need to explain the importance of the task as enthusiastically as possible, before proceeding with the minimum of fuss.

Teachers need to help pupils make connections with previous work

A series of disjointed sessions can lead to frustration and attempts by pupils to make sense of things for themselves by asking numerous questions, making speculative comments or, in the worst cases, wilful resistance. All these actions acts against a positive classroom climate and may result in teachers suppressing the verbal communication.

Explaining to pupils why something is being done is not the same as justifying it to them

There is little to gain, and much to lose, by adopting a 'pleading' type of approach as though to ask the pupils' permission. Although it is helpful to spend a short time placing the learning in context for pupils and enthusing about why it is important, it is very unhelpful wasting time going into unnecessary detail about every small part of every lesson.

Teachers have to decide how much information to give pupils prior to the task and how much to allow pupils to find out for themselves

This has to be explained carefully so that pupils are not in any doubt about the ground-rules for the task. Pupils need to know if everyone is doing the same thing at the same time or whether they are to work singly, with a partner or in groups. It has to be made clear to them whether they are allowed to select their partners, work with the person/people nearest to them or move position and work in a group to which they are allocated by the teacher. Teachers need to explain where the task is to be carried out and how much autonomy pupils are allowed in making decisions about practical issues to do with the most appropriate way of getting the job completed.

Teachers need to have the necessary resources available and ensure that pupils know how to use them correctly and sensibly

Pupils must be told about any relevant routines or procedures, such as who has first use of equipment, who is responsible for it, and what happens after they have finished with it. Spelling out the procedural factors oils the wheels of lesson management.

Pupils should be told how long they have to complete the task

Teachers should take into account the different abilities and speeds of working within the group or class, and what will be done about incomplete work at the end of the session.

Pupils need to be informed about what will happen to their completed work

For instance, whether it is for private use or public display, and the criteria the teacher will be using to assess its value. Teachers should encourage the pupils to set their own standards and ensure that they know what form of help and support will be available during the session.

Much of the above information, explanation and clarification described above can be administered at the start of the lesson; however, opportunities within the main body of the lesson should be utilised for reminders about procedures, enthusing about progress, and reminding pupils of the required standards.

Communicative networks

There are many ways in which verbal communication can be used to enhance the learning situation. Edwards and Furlong (1978) claim that there are six 'participant structures' that may take place in classrooms. A participant structure 'refers to typical arrangements of speakers and listeners...communicative networks linking those who are in contact with one another already or can be if they choose'. The list in the table below is based on Edwards and Furlong's original propositions:

Table 10

Communicative networks (after Edwards and Furlong, 1978)

- *When the teacher talks to a silent audience and requires everyone's attention.*
- *When the teacher talks directly to one pupil but assumes that everyone else is attending to what is being said.*
- *When one or more pupils and the teacher talk together while the rest of the class listen.*
- *When the teacher talks to one or more pupils while the rest of the class discuss their own work independently.*
- *When the pupils discuss among themselves with the teacher chairing.*
- *When pupils discuss among themselves without the teacher's involvement.*

For convenience, the following section deals with the propositions under three broad headings:

- when only the teacher talks;
- individual teacher-pupil interactions;
- group discussion.

When only the teacher talks

The situation in which the teacher addresses the whole class at the same time is sometimes referred to as didactic, transmission or direct teaching (see also Chapter 4). Transmission teaching is very common at all stages of schooling, though it is generally more favoured in work with older pupils. Although the teacher assumes that each pupil is listening and receiving what is said, experience suggests that this assumption may be optimistic. Pupils may be silent because they are concentrating or because they daydreaming or half asleep! The disadvantage of one teacher addressing a large number of pupils lies not only in having one voice speaking and lots of different ears listening, but in the fact that each brain interprets the words differently.

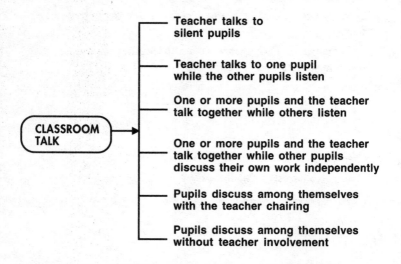

CLASSROOM TALK

- Teacher talks to silent pupils
- Teacher talks to one pupil while the other pupils listen
- One or more pupils and the teacher talk together while others listen
- One or more pupils and the teacher talk together while other pupils discuss their own work independently
- Pupils discuss among themselves with the teacher chairing
- Pupils discuss among themselves without teacher involvement

Figure 10 – *Forms of classroom talk (after Edwards and Furlong, 1978)*

The more the pupils are similar in ability, the more focused the teacher's words can be and the less time has to be spent on explanations, rehearsal of ideas and revision of concepts.

Although direct transmission from teacher to pupil often forms part of a lesson, it is unusual for the whole lesson to consist of this single approach. Didactic teaching is necessarily accompanied by some form of monitoring process, such as asking pupils questions or providing an activity which tests understanding of the earlier part of the lesson.

Individual teacher–pupil and pupil–teacher interactions

In a whole class interactive session that often follows transmission teaching, there are occasions when the teacher speaks to an individual pupil with the remainder of the class silently listening to the interaction (often in the form of question-and-answer). On other occasions, teachers set pupils suitable tasks and activities once they have completed their transmission teaching. As soon as the pupils have settled and teachers are free to move around the room, they will inevitably begin to intervene in their pupils' work, ask questions, offer advice or give pupils an opportunity to share their ideas or findings. The majority of conversations between the teacher and pupil have to take place on the assumption that the remainder of the class are getting on with their own work. If teachers sometimes find that they are repeating things to a number of pupils, it is worth them asking the class to stop what they are doing and addressing them all about the point of interest at the same time. In this way, all pupils benefit from the knowledge and insights that are emerging from the one-to-one verbal contact. The teacher may feel that it is appropriate to use the single participant interaction as a stimulus for a wider debate and a more inclusive discussion.

Inexperienced teachers are particularly prone to enjoying an intimate exchange with one or two selected pupils, oblivious to the fact that others in the class have lost interest in what they are doing. When these teachers eventually become aware of the situation, they rebuke the restless pupils, yet are largely responsible for the problem because of their own poor management.

As we have already considered, it is unusual for a verbal interaction to be <u>initiated</u> by a pupil unless it is to seek help with work or the teacher has sanctioned the strategy. If one pupil speaks while others listen, it will normally be in response to a teacher question or offering a contribution to a teacher-initiated discussion.

Group discussion

Pupil discussion in groups is worthwhile for a number of reasons, including:

- It allows pupils to engage with the subject in hand.
- It obliges pupils to think for themselves.
- It offers an opportunity for pupils to express their own ideas publicly.
- It gives pupils access to other peoples' ideas and understanding.
- It helps pupils to recognise that there are valid opinions other than their own..
- It brings members of a group closer together.
- It combines the wisdom, knowledge and experience of many.

Group discussions have become increasingly accepted as an important part of the learning process and take place under two circumstances.

In small groups of four or five pupils

Small group problem solving typically involves the teacher introducing an issue or problem that would benefit from the collective wisdom of every member of the group. This 'two heads are better than one' approach to learning has become increasingly popular as teachers have recognised the advantages of involving pupils in purposeful discussions. Having established the conditions for the task, the teacher remains detached from the process unless invited by the group to offer comment or advice.

Autonomous pupil discussions require considerable preparation, both in structuring the collaborative task and in teaching pupils the necessary skills for group membership. Teachers may be tempted to believe that arranging for pupils to discuss among themselves provides an easy option; in truth, the preparation and follow-up procedures place heavy demands upon both teacher and taught.

As a whole class

A common example of the latter is in the growth of shared times such as 'circle time' (for example, Currie and Bromfield, 1998) in which pupils are invited to contribute within a safe and positive environment while sitting or seated in a circle, able to see one another comfortably and make comments within a supportive environment. Teachers of younger children frequently use these occasions to discuss relationship issues, make decisions about classroom procedures, celebrate success and raise self-esteem through receiving spoken affirmatory comments.

Talk can be generated through group work tasks that have been structured by the teacher but in which the pupils are given opportunity to <u>share their findings</u>. For instance:

- Pupils are asked to sort and group objects, propositions, events or other assorted facts and justify their selection to the rest of the class.
- Pupils explore the conditions which resulted in a particular outcome and provide the general rule framework governing the circumstances. This activity is especially relevant to science and historical events. It provides opportunity for pupils to look beyond the immediate circumstances and generalise findings.

The best forms of reporting back allow for other pupils to comment constructively on what has been said.

Activity 32

1. Incorporate a report-back phase into lessons in which collaborative group work forms a key element.

2. Following each group's report, leave a minute or two for other groups to decide on a constructive comment.

3. Give opportunity for the groups to make their comments before moving on to another group's report-back.

4. Incorporate all the comments in your final summary.

The importance of group work in learning is sufficiently important to devote a further section on examining the factors impinging upon the organisation of groups.

Organising groups

The composition of groups will depend to some extent on what we are trying to achieve through the lesson or series of lessons and the most effective means for accomplishing it. Central to this decision is determining the way in which grouping pupils will facilitate the desired learning outcomes:

- by helping pupils to work with others co-operatively;
- by helping pupils to work with others collaboratively.

Table II

A comparison of co-operation and collaboration

Co-operative working

- *part of a larger socialising function, especially with younger pupils;*
- *assumes egalitarianism (no hierarchy);*
- *appropriate for major projects and team activities.*

Collaborative working

- *requires a common purpose;*
- *all members need to contribute;*
- *roles within the group may have to be allocated;*
- *appropriate for problem-solving, investigative, open-ended tasks.*

There are also implications for <u>classroom management</u>:

- When there is a limited amount of equipment, group work may have to be staggered across several sessions, with other pupils engaged in different activities while they await their turn.

- Monitoring of pupils who are working with limited resources is essential. In practice, this means that certain collaborative activities can only go ahead when there is additional adult support available (such as a classroom assistant).

- Group size must not only be considered from a learning perspective but from a practical one, such as how many pupils can fit into a given area.

Activity 33

1. Change the pattern of grouping for a lesson based on ideas noted above and assess the impact upon the level of verbal interaction within them, using the following as a guide:

- the free flow of ideas in the groups;
- the time it takes for pupils to adjust to the new conditions;
- the noise level;
- the learning dynamics;
- the number of complaints from pupils about other pupils.

2. Evaluate the success of the lesson using the 'four factors':

- learning better together than apart;
- facilitating co-operation and/or collaboration;
- pupils' speaking and listening skills;
- monitoring and assessing progress.

In any form of collaborative venture in which verbal communication is central to reaching successful outcomes, we also need to take account of the following two points.

The noise level

- larger groups generally make more noise than smaller ones;
- some open-ended tasks require a lot of talk;
- talk can be mis-directed unless there is close teacher supervision;
- assertive children can dominate groups of all sizes.

The teacher's role during group work

- to concentrate on a single group;
- to wander and monitor children's progress;
- to sit and watch;
- to contribute as a group member.

Eliciting responses

For teachers who are convinced that raising the level of pupils' verbal participation will result in more effective learning, the success with which they achieve their purposes depends largely upon their ability to elicit suitable contributions from as many pupils as possible. The process by which this is achieved can be broadly divided into those strategies in which the talk is initiated by the teacher and those which rely upon pupils' initiative. This section deals with the different demands made of pupils through teacher-initiated talk.

Nuthall and Lawrence (1965) suggested that teacher-initiated verbal interaction with pupils can be categorised using 'cognitive operations'. The forms of responses illustrated below are based on some of Nuthall and Lawrence's original propositions but have been re-classified and interpreted. Note that they follow a commonly experienced action-reaction pattern in which the teacher 'acts' and the pupil 'reacts'. The two broad categories are:

- Teacher-initiated talk with a pre-determined expectation.
- Teacher-initiated talk without pre-condition.

Teacher initiated talk with a pre-determined expectation

This teaching approach assumes that the teacher has decided what constitutes an appropriate response in advance of asking a question. There are four common forms.

Defining

Pupils are asked by the teacher to explain the meaning of a word, expression, concept or specific term. The teacher evaluates the accuracy of the answer and confirms the correctness or otherwise of the pupil's definition.

Describing

Pupils are asked to give an account of (say) a happening, a geographical location or an incident. The teacher takes account of the content of the reply and the pupils' ability to express themselves concisely.

Designating

Pupils have to give a single word answer to a question about something or someone. Designating typically involves closed forms of questions in which there is only one correct answer. The teacher has to decide how many answers to receive before confirming the correct one. The alternative is to avoid the need for spending time on seeing who knows the answer, and <u>telling</u> them instead.

Substituting

Pupils are asked to manipulate information that is given by the teacher, such as in a mathematical calculation. The teacher is interested in the accuracy of pupils' answers, but equally in their ability to explain how they reached them. The pupils' language usage will offer clues about their conceptual understanding.

Valuing mistakes

Forms of questions in which there are pre-conditions are usually more suitable for reminding pupils of earlier work than for introducing new topics. Although teachers commonly ask questions with an expectation about what constitutes a satisfactory answer, it is important to take note of the value of mistakes:

1. Some apparently incorrect answers may be as a result of misunderstanding or misinformation rather than knowledge or conceptual deficit.

2. In their eagerness to supply an answer, some pupils do not give sufficiently careful thought to what they say.

3. Mistakes can be a valuable source of debate and reflection if used positively.

4. Correct answers do not necessarily reveal much about a pupil's deeper understanding of the processes involved in determining the answer.

Teachers should be aware that asking questions with a pre-condition places power with the adult. The only reward for the pupil is to be approved for answering correctly. One reason that team games are so popular with younger children is that it gives all pupils a chance to be part of a successful enterprise.

Teacher initiated talk without pre-condition

The value of teacher initiated talk in which there are few, if any, pre-conditions, is that pupils can contribute their ideas without the anxieties which attach to those questions with a pre-determined answer. Teachers can accommodate the most sensible responses into the discussion and encourage a higher degree of participation. The expression 'without pre-conditions' is slightly misleading as it conveys the idea that any answer or comment is acceptable. In fact, the nature of the question will establish some constraints on what is said, depending on how the question is framed, pupils' previous encounters with the curriculum content being explored and their existing knowledge. There are five common forms.

Stating

- **Pupils** are invited to give their views about issues and proposals an extended verbal response.
- **Teachers** offer appropriate support through positive body language, gestures and affirming comments.

Evaluating

- **Pupils** offer opinions about the appropriateness of an action, situation or event. They may, for instance, summarise events or comment upon the quality of a written text.
- **Teachers** hope to hear a balanced viewpoint, supported by relevant evidence.

Inferring

- **Pupils** make inferences from existing evidence. Whereas evaluating deals with the present reality, inferring gives opportunity to give an opinion about future possibilities.
- **Teachers** evaluate the extent to which the predictions take sufficient account of present trends and creative possibilities.

Comparing and contrasting

- **Pupils** have to explain the differences between things and their similarities, using common characteristics or features, and justify their choices.

- **Teachers** take note of the sharpness of pupils' perceptions, the vocabulary used to describe the differences, and their ability to select significant factors.

Conditional inferring

- **Pupils** are given information and asked to comment upon the suggested outcome or offer an alternative one. Typically, the question will commence with: 'Suppose that...'. Sufficient information needs to be given for pupils to offer a well-informed evaluation, though some points may have to be clarified.

- **Teachers** anticipate that pupils will offer a wide range of views, but must demand that each view is properly justified and reasoned.

The teacher's role in initiating talk without pre-condition is to offer pupils as much opportunity as possible to express their ideas clearly and convincingly. Some pupils may struggle to articulate their thoughts and may require additional time if they are to develop their verbal communication skills. However, the best place to enhance these skills is in the relative security of a small group rather than in front of the whole class.

Activity 34

1. Determine which of the five categories (stating/evaluating/inferring/comparing and contrasting/conditional inferring) you intend to incorporate into a lesson, and their impact upon pupils' learning.

2. Reflect upon ways in which you might assist pupils in communicating their ideas more succinctly and meaningfully by providing supportive comments, recapitulation of the key points and incorporation of their comments into the overall learning framework.

3. Evaluate the impact upon pupils' learning using the following criteria on the scale: **Strong/Satisfactory/Weak/Problematic**.

- level of enthusiasm;
- control problems;
- grasp of the lesson principles;
- verbal contributions;
- use of vocabulary;
- attention to task.

Lesson phases

Different phases of a lesson make different demands upon the teacher's communicative abilities (see the table below).

Table 12

Demands made on teachers' communicative abilities

- *The introductory phase entails holding the attention of the whole class.*
- *After task allocation has taken place, communication with pupils concerns the on-going work.*
- *The latter part of lesson may necessitate handling pupils' report-backs, summarising findings and drawing conclusions.*
- *The final moments of a lesson are often spent commenting on work, commending, rebuking, extending thinking and predicting links with future sessions.*

Some lessons are very specifically designed. For instance, the Literacy Hour (DfEE, 1997) requires that primary teachers teach explicitly within a carefully structured hour long session, the majority of which should be directly focused whole class teaching. Many lessons involve a mixture of transmission teaching and an interactive phase (involving discussion, debate and brainstorming), followed by individual tasks or group work (including problem solving, investigation or other practical activities) Teachers need to utilise a range of verbal interactive skills during a single lesson; but pupils also have to draw on a number of skills to respond to the teacher's demands. Thus:

- The **teacher** uses transmission teaching.

  The **pupils** need listening skills.

- The **teacher** invites comments and ideas.

  The **pupils** have to express their thinking in words.

- The **teacher** explains the organisation and tasks for group activities.

  The **pupils** have to interpret the task and contribute towards the collaborative venture.

- The **teacher** asks for feedback and comments.

  The **pupils** have to synthesise their ideas and offer a summary.

Teachers have to be clear about the lesson structure, whether their proposed approach is manageable and how much time needs to be spent inculcating the class into the necessary routines, rules and procedures (see the table below).

Table 13

Considerations in lesson planning

Teachers should:

- *be clear about the structure of individual lessons and the dominant forms of verbal interaction they propose to use throughout the lesson;*
- *be confident that opportunities for verbal interaction are adequately planned;*
- *give careful consideration to the manageability of their proposed structures;*
- *be convinced that the verbal strategies they favour lead to the most effective learning outcomes for pupils;*
- *be aware of pupils' previous experience of involvement in different forms of participation and not assume that they are capable of making best use of opportunities, simply because they are offered to them.*

Inadequate thought to the management of the types of verbal interaction explored above can lead to an unsatisfactory working atmosphere, punctuated by constant queries about procedures, demands for explanations about the tasks, a high noise level and general frustration as pupils struggle to understand what the teacher is trying to accomplish, and by what means.

Classroom layout

There are practical issues about teacher-pupil verbal interaction which depend upon the classroom layout, grouping of pupils and position of the teacher in the room. For instance, during transmission teaching, the formal layout shown in Figure 11 may be most appropriate, depending on whether whether we need access to a fixed point, such as a board or overhead projector. If a more reciprocal style is being used, in which the teacher initiates the discourse and pupils respond accordingly, the layout shown in Figure 12 allows us a clear view of all the pupils. If we want to encourage fuller pupil participation, Figure 13 facilitates an interactive mode of working, allowing us to see and interact with the pupils, and the pupils to do so with one another. It not only makes it possible for pupils to discuss things together without turning and straining their necks, but helps us to monitor progress with the minimum of movement about the room. During group work activities, the layout in Figure 14 is best suited to the learning conditions as it puts pupils in sets of about four, and offers us the physical space to moderate proceedings.

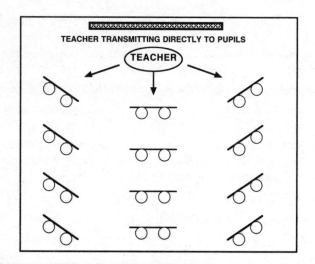

TEACHER TRANSMITTING DIRECTLY TO PUPILS

TEACHER

Figure 11 – *Class layout for transmission teaching*

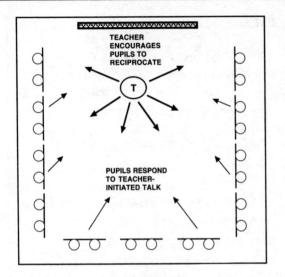

Figure 12 – *Class layout for reciprocal teaching*

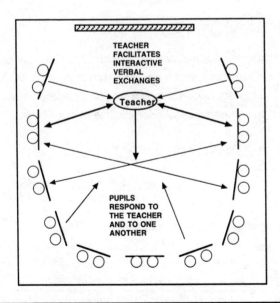

Figure 13 – *Class layout for interactive teaching*

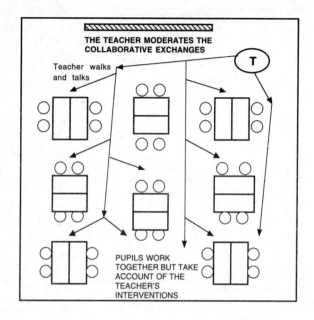

Figure 14 – Class layout for collaborative activities

Different patterns of verbal interaction are facilitated by particular classroom arrangements. However, space constraints, visibility of aids and health and safety factors also impinge upon decisions concerning the style of classroom layout used for any lesson (see Hayes, 1997).

Reading aloud

There are a number of factors to take into account when reading aloud.

The physical position of teacher and class

- If good eye contact is considered important, pupils need to be located in such a way that teachers can look up from the text and engage the pupils visually without losing their place.
- If it helps for the text to be visible to pupils (such as using 'big books' with beginner readers), a closer position is needed than if pupils have a copy of their own text in front of them.

Tone and intonation

- Whatever the physical constraints, the principles of clear speech explored in earlier chapters, such as stressing key words, dramatising passages, pacing and pausing and so on) have to be maintained.

- The pause is particularly important when reading aloud, because it gives listeners a chance to absorb the mood of the text and allows teachers an opportunity to collect their thoughts and remain calmer than would be the case were they to gabble through what had to be said.

Acting

- To some extent all teaching is a form of acting. However, there are occasions when a little melodrama adds to the interest level of what is being read aloud and engages pupils' emotions more keenly than speaking in a regular way.

- The quality and variation in tone results in a greater variety of shading in the voice which, in turn, may elicit a more active response in pupils.

- There may be occasions when it is worth telling rather than reading, providing all the necessary information is conveyed to the pupils. This obviously requires additional preparation and planning (Jones and Buttrey, 1970).

The use of visual aids

- Visual aids (pictures, photographs, puppets and models for example) provide a useful support for reading aloud, but also involve a number of practical challenges for the teacher in handling them.

- Nevertheless, the availability of visual material can help to transform an otherwise mundane session into something more imaginative.

Chapter 6

Motivation and class control

Well had the boding tremblers learned to trace, the day's disasters in his morning face.

(Oliver Goldsmith, The Village Schoolmaster)

One thing we nearly all have in common is that we went to school and encountered a variety of people who were paid to teach us. It is almost certain that these teachers varied considerably in the impact they had upon our learning and our attitude to schooling in general. The majority were decent, hard-working people who made a good job of teaching us. A few were outstanding and memorable, either because they were able to inspire us about their subject or, due to their personality and inter-personal skills, were able to transform even the dullest session into something tolerable. A few were hopeless because they could not keep control and resorted to shouting, punishments or aggressive comments to maintain some semblance of order.

The impact of teachers upon the pupils they teach

Although the sights and sounds of school life quickly fade, it is common to hear reminiscences about particular events, special occasions or individual encounters which remain fixed in a person's memory and occasionally surface in animated conversation about the old days.

Most young children seem to enjoy a satisfactory relationship with their teacher. Older pupils are less tolerant, loving some teachers and loathing others. Certain teachers remain imprinted upon our memories because of their warmth and friendly manner. We can still hear the harsh and accusatory tones of others. One way or another, teachers influenced our attitude to school and learning in general.

In fifty years time, when the pupils we teach are grandparents and asked by their own grandchildren to tell them about their teachers when they were at school, what will they remember about us?

The power of the tongue

There are occasions when teachers fall prey to using words as weapons. Speech becomes a poisoned chalice instead of a medium for communication, and conversation deteriorates into verbal skirmishes rather than constructive dialogue. When the pressure of teaching is at its most intense, even the best teachers are inclined to resort to demands and threats rather than invitations and suggestions. There are times, of course, when strong speaking is necessary, but verbal loss of control can lead to things being said that should not have been uttered, and the complaints or protests from pupils or parents that sometimes arise as a result.

It is not, of course, the words alone which carry meaning for the listener, but the way in which they are spoken and in which they are supported by the teacher's actions. Pupils quickly become disillusioned and feel cheated if a teacher says one thing and does another, or never gets around to fulfilling promises.

Pupils, too, are capable of speaking in ways which create distress for the teacher and other pupils. A healthy verbal environment needs active agreement between teachers and pupils about the parameters for talk – what is allowable and what is not. It is when teachers or (more commonly) pupils disregard or deliberately infringe the agreed rules, that it becomes difficult to maintain a high quality communicative ethos.

It is counter-productive for teachers to respond to pupils' unsatisfactory comments by being even more unpleasant.

The verbal climate

The best learning environments are those in which pupils are encouraged to express themselves, but in which any talk which is personally hurtful or negative is censored. A <u>positive</u> verbal climate is one in which teachers are approachable, good listeners and willing to be patient when pupils struggle to express themselves or offer an unpopular opinion. Pupils are invited to contribute their ideas but are not pressurised unduly. There is a sensible balance of interactive talk involving the whole class, and small group collaborative work for pupils to discuss ideas, establish a position or otherwise synthesise their thinking.

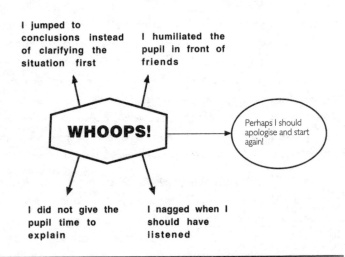

Figure 15 – Unhelpful responses

The <u>worst</u> learning environments, and those which induce resentment or wilful behaviour, are those characterised by teachers who rely upon humiliation, accusation and nagging, instead of reasoned comment and persuasion. Such teachers showed obvious dislike for certain pupils, leading to feelings of unfairness, inequality of opportunity and, in extreme cases, betrayal. The teachers struggle to develop any meaningful relationship with the class, so subject the pupils to a barrage of teacher-talk, and minimise opportunities for pupils to offer ideas or opinions. Pupil uncertainty is met with derision; stereotyped answers are unduly praised, and there is little incentive for creative thinking. Collaborative group activity is rarely employed; pupil-pupil verbal exchanges are considered threatening, so the teachers respond with hectoring rebukes and personal insult.

Knowing ourselves

As we consider the sort of effective verbal strategies that we might employ in dealing with control issues and motivating our pupils, it helps us to understand what kind of teacher we are. Smith (1993) suggests that there are three broad types:

- an **authoritarian** teacher;
- a **decisive** teacher;
- an **indecisive** teacher.

An **authoritarian** teacher sees power over pupils as an end in itself and will use embarrassment and humiliation to gain and sustain this power. It is an 'us' and 'them' situation in which the teacher must win at all costs. Teachers prefers to blame the pupils rather than examine their own style of teaching or personal manner when things go wrong.

A **decisive** teacher negotiates and develops rules with pupils. The teacher acknowledges that some minor disruption is inevitable from time to time and adopts positive techniques to address the situation. The teacher uses humour and occasional repartee and enjoys informal conversations with the pupils. These teachers are brief, calm, assertive and avoid nagging their pupils.

An **indecisive** teacher knows what to do but not how to go about it. The teacher is insufficiently assertive and allows pupils to dominate proceedings and create their own classroom rules. The teacher often enters into fruitless dialogue with disruptive pupils rather than issuing direct statements and commands. The teacher feels under constant pressure.

Smith suggests that it is possible to allocate teachers to one of the above categories on the basis of their responses. It is important to note in passing that self perception does not necessarily equate with the reality of classroom practice. Teachers' intentions of the way they think they are acting and pupils' perceptions of the classroom are sometimes markedly different. For instance, whereas teachers may intend to give pupils responsibility for their own actions and decisions, the reality is sometimes quite different. Nevertheless, Smith's model is a helpful means of examining how aspects of verbal interaction impinge upon class control and discipline issues. **Authoritarianism** is associated with seven characteristics (see the table below).

Table 14

Characteristics of an authoritarian teacher

- *demanding (as opposed to requesting)*
- *telling (as opposed to empowering)*
- *harsh tones (as opposed to level ones)*
- *threatening (as opposed to reasoning)*
- *stereotyped phrases (as opposed to tailored ones)*
- *nagging (as opposed to explaining)*
- *hostility (as opposed to resolution)*

Clearly, a teacher who employed such verbal strategies would monopolise the talk, grant limited opportunity for dialogue and use words for chastising rather than crafting. As Tough (1985) neatly puts it: 'Talk in the classroom may be so much concerned with control that the children may never experience talk that might extend their thinking'.

An **indecisive** teacher is likely to be characterised by five characteristics (see the table below).

Table 15

Characteristics of an indecisive teacher

- *passivity (as opposed to assertiveness)*
- *extensive dialogue (as opposed to limited dialogue)*
- *hesitant tone (as opposed to confident tone)*
- *angry remarks (as opposed to controlled ones)*
- *submissive manner (as opposed to firm manner)*

Finally, the **decisive** teacher adopts verbal strategies that we would instantly recognise as ideal (see the table below).

Table 16

Characteristics of a decisive teacher

- *direct and assertive communication*
- *respectful tone (even when angry)*
- *non-judgemental*
- *clear, firm and polite speech*

A close examination of the above characteristics also reveals that characteristic patterns of speech are closely associated with particular attitudes about the learning process and teacher-pupil relationships. The key feature of **authoritarian** teachers is that they do not allow for individual differences. The **indecisive** teacher is unsure about whether it is right to tell pupils what to do and feels guilty; the **decisive** teacher separates the person from the behaviour.

> *Effective teachers are those who are able to reach out to pupils, to appreciate and understand their needs, and seek specific and individual ways of satisfying them.*
>
> *(Whitaker, 1997)*

Submissive, aggressive or assertive?

Bolton (1979) makes a helpful distinction between submissive, assertive and aggressive behaviour. He suggests that listening and assertion are interdependent and complementary. The most effective communication is only possible when teachers are willing to listen and to adopt an assertive approach to classroom order. Thus:

- **Submissive** behaviour is typical of those who want to be liked by others; although submissive people initially gain many friends, if the behaviour dominates their lives, they soon become the object of scorn and even disgust.

- **Aggressive** people get their own way by exercising direct control over their own lives and those of others; however, dominant people often become alienated and disillusioned.

- **Assertive** behaviour deals with the immediate situation in a non-threatening, specific way, and does not attempt to avoid the problem by nitpicking about an associated issue. Assertive people do not use their speech to condemn or accuse, but rather to address situations and examine the principles or actions, rather than the individual concerned.

Activity 35

Sub-divide the following six teacher statements under the three headings: **submissive**, **aggressive** and **assertive**.

1. Your trouble is that you are too full of yourself.

2. I'd quite like it if you were a bit quieter.

3. For goodness sake, sit down and stop messing about with that stupid bit of string.

4. Please put the book back on the shelf and line up with the others.

5. Please don't bang the table; it disturbs everyone in the room.

6. Shh-hh; shh-hh.

Numbers 1 and 3 are **aggressive** remarks. Numbers 2 and 6 are **submissive** comments. Numbers 4 and 5 are **assertive** comments.

The way in which we phrase the same ideas is important if we want to communicate assertively. For instance, the first of the comments below is **submissive**; the second is **aggressive**; the third is **assertive**. Yet they are all trying to achieve the same purpose:

Submissive

'Last time when you put your trays away, you were rather noisy, so this time I'd like you to try very hard to do your best and put them away without making too much noise, please.'

Aggressive

'Put your trays away; do it now; if I hear anyone banging them about I shall be very cross because I'm fed up with people like you, Abigail, trying to shove them into the trolley like a silly baby.'

Assertive

'In a few moments I shall ask you to put your trays away. Please check that they are tidy first. When you are satisfied that things are in order, slide your tray into the trolley as carefully as you can, then sit in your seat and show me that you are ready.'

Activity 36

Consider the verbal response you might make in the following circumstances under the three main headings: **submissive**, **aggressive**, **assertive**:

- A girl has snatched a pencil from another child and they are arguing about ownership.
- A boy is moving across the room, deliberately banging into tables and pretending to be dizzy.
- Despite your careful explanation, a normally sensible girl has written her work in pencil instead of ink.
- During a science lesson, two boys have made earrings out of the crocodile clips and are showing off to their friends.
- A boy burps loudly in the middle of a lesson and immediately, but unconvincingly, apologises.

- A boy is doodling on some scrap paper during your whole class explanation.
- Pupils come in noisily after playtime.
- A boy and girl squabble about who goes last in the queue.
- A group of three pupils are chattering about a TV programme rather than the work.
- A girl is quietly eating her snack during the lesson.
- A truculent child tells you that his dad says that he doesn't have to do what you tell him.

It is worth persevering with assertive speech rather than relying on the submissive or aggressive forms, as it leads to fewer control problems and more highly motivated pupils in the long term. Aggressive and submissive speech may result in short-term gains but generally depress a healthy, interactive classroom climate.

Activity 37

Evaluate your own approach to control issues with reference to the following criteria using the scale **Strong characteristic/ Satisfactory characteristic/Unsatisfactory characteristic**:

1. Thinking through your verbal strategies in advance rather than relying wholly on spontaneous or instinctive reactions.

2. Ignoring unsuitable behaviour where possible but make the pupil aware of your displeasure through non-verbal signals.

3. Making it clear that you will not tolerate rudeness or insolence.

4. Issuing direct, polite and firm statements.

5. Using pupils' names to gain their attention, not as a focus for personal insult.

6. Reminding the pupil of the agreed conventions for verbal behaviour.

7. Asking pupils to explain what they are doing, and ask them what they ought to be doing.

8. Insisting that pupils face up to their responsibility rather than blaming others.

9. Dealing with pupils' genuine concerns as soon as possible.

||| **10.** Thanking a pupil who resumes appropriate behaviour.
||| **11.** Stating sanctions as facts rather than threats.

Speech conventions

The most important consideration in any discourse is that speakers convey their ideas clearly and genuinely.

Implicit and explicit speech

It pays to say what we mean. Introducing innuendo and veiled meanings to what they say may give teachers a personal thrill but is unlikely to cut much ice with pupils who want clarity of meaning. In particular, it takes young children some time to realise that there is a second order (implicit) meaning attached to what the teacher is saying. Over time, younger children learn to interpret their teacher's words and understand that there are subtle meanings attached to many statements. In the meantime, teachers should be wary of using expressions and statements that are understood by adults but bewildering to inexperienced pupils.

Even when the teacher is attempting to be explicit, the same words can have different meanings in different contexts. For instance, the commonly used assertion: 'Everybody sit down' can have different meanings, depending upon the context:

- In the **classroom** this statement may be used to denote that there is too much fuss or movement about the room (that is, as a control strategy).
- In a **large space** activity it might be used as precursor to an exciting activity (that is, as the first statement in a sequence of events).

In the **classroom**, the teacher might follow the statement with 'That's a lot better; now get on with your work more quietly. You have got to have your investigation completed by 12 o'clock.'

In the **large space**, further statements might include: 'Well done; now I'm going to put you in groups for the drama work', followed by 'After I shake the tambourine, I want you to stand up very slowly and move towards others in your group. Remember that you are on a very large planet and the gravitational pull makes it impossible to move quickly.' In the circumstances of working in a large space, the original statement is subsequently used as a precursor to a subtle control strategy (moving slowly) but the purpose of the first statement is to do with pedagogy rather than discipline.

Similarly, when a teacher says: 'It would be nice to have a bit of hush!' this is not merely a statement of fact, but an attempt to restore classroom order. If a pupil were to respond with: 'I agree with you' the teacher would consider this as insolence rather than support. The 'shh-hh' so beloved of younger pupils that sometimes follows the teacher's pronouncement indicates that some of them, at least, understand the implications of what is said. Generally, it is better to use a direct statement such as: 'Please work more quietly' than a vague: 'It would be nice to have a bit of hush' as the former gives a clear directive that can be monitored, whereas the latter is open to interpretation and will probably have to be followed by a direct command anyway.

Experienced teachers tend to use more direct commands than inexperienced teachers, but only when they are reasonably certain that they will be obeyed. Inexperienced teachers may think that a direct command (especially delivered in a firm tone) will achieve the required behaviour automatically. However, pupils will disregard or deliberately re-interpret the direct instruction if they resent teachers or do not recognise their status. Student teachers have a particular problem in this regard, as pupils perceive that they are not 'real' ones. Although it requires a great deal of determination and courage for students to convince them otherwise, it is worth persevering with explicit rather than implicit statements.

Activity 38

1. Use the tape recording that you made in Activity 5.3 to assess the explicitness of your statements to pupils.

2. Select three or four key statements which seem to lack explicitness and write down a better alternative.

3. Gradually incorporate the alternative phrasing into future lessons.

4. Continue the process by taking one example each day and improving its explicitness.

Use of humour

Teacher humour is a valuable asset in maintaining class control; however, it is not just a question of when and where to use humour but of how it is interpreted by the pupils. Some teachers may be tempted to use humour to placate pupils or create an artificially intimate atmosphere. Such tactics are not advised as pupils resent weak-willed teachers and quickly see through any attempt to circumvent the difficult task of establishing control by creating a mood of revelry. A little humour is a useful antidote to any inclination to become too serious, but should arise naturally when the teacher-pupil relationships have become secure. Jokes are best left to comedians. Unacceptable forms of humour include taunting, teasing and tormenting.

Excessive classroom humour can easily lead to things getting out of control and pupils begin to take up the jokey theme and impress their own brand of humour on the situation, beginning with wisecracks and progressing to ribald remarks and vulgarity. Younger pupils enjoy telling a joke to their teacher and the majority of them are harmless.

If an older pupil offers to tell a joke, it may be wiser to decline. However, if we do listen to a joke that proves to be unsuitable, either because it is vulgar or cruel, the best response is no response: 'Sorry, I just don't find that funny'. It is unlikely that we will be bothered again.

Lesson stages

Teachers need to clarify for pupils what is allowable during particular stages of the lesson. For instance:

- Only the teacher is allowed to talk.
- Teacher talk will be followed by questions.
- Pupils can interrupt if they first raise their hand and are invited.
- Pupils can interrupt at any time, providing they obey conversation conventions.

Teachers have got to be as clear about the structure of their classroom talk as they have about their learning intentions if they are to avoid the worst excesses of pupil interruptions, remarks and low concentration levels. If pupils are being encouraged to speak, the procedures for taking turns and responding to points that arise must be clearly understood or time will be wasted in constant explanations and rebukes for transgressions. Properly managed talk facilitates learning; poorly managed talk hinders it due to the unhelpful ebbs and flows in the verbal interaction patterns and the control problems that are created.

Interpreting pupils' actions

It is tempting for a teacher to assume that pupils' actions are due to unco-operativeness rather than incorrect interpretation of what teachers intended. Although some speech seems unequivocal, it is always worth thinking hard about the meaning that words convey. For example, if Mr Allan says to a pupil: 'Elaine, please shut the window', Elaine will make one of several responses:

- she will immediately shut the window;
- she will wait for a short time and shut the window;
- she will shut the window and make a disturbance while doing so;
- she will not shut the window at all.

Although we may consider that Mr Allan's statement cannot be misinterpreted and that only the first response is satisfactory, each action tells us something about the way in which his words have been received (see the table on page 127).

Table 17

Interpreting a pupil's actions

- *Elaine heard and understood the command and made the action a priority.*
- *Elaine heard and understood the command but did not consider that the action was a priority. (Perhaps she was in the middle of a sentence or did not hear the voice tone which required <u>immediate</u> action.)*
- *Elaine heard and understood the command but felt that the request was unreasonable or was disdainful of the teacher's right to exercise authority.*
- *Elaine did not hear the teacher or chose to ignore him.*

Mr Allan's own response to Elaine's actions will depend on what he intended when he made the comment:

- If he meant that shutting the window was a priority, he could have added: '...only the wind is blowing the paper off the desk'.
- If he did not consider the action to be a priority, he could have added: '...as soon as you've got a moment', conveying to Elaine that although the action was necessary, he trusted her to make the decision about the timing.
- If he was merely exercising his authority over Elaine, he can hardly have been surprised by her reaction.
- If he did not expect Elaine to obey the command, he would have done better to close the window himself!

To a large extent, pupils' responses will depend upon their disposition and age. Primary pupils often see an opportunity to please the teacher as a privilege and delight. Older pupils may be less compliant. Nevertheless, the same principle of the teacher thinking carefully about the intended action, and being as specific as possible in translating that thought into speech, applies to every situation.

Dealing with interruptions

If pupils interrupt at an inappropriate time, teachers have a number of options, depending upon whether the conventions for interrupting have been obeyed, and whether the comment or question is genuine or contrived. If the interruption is **unauthorised**, the teacher has three options:

To ignore the comment

This may be effective with older pupils who are likely to correctly interpret a lack of response and negative body language. A simple non-verbal signal (such as a raised palm) may be sufficient to allow teachers to continue their flow of words without pausing. Otherwise, a request for the pupil to wait for a moment allows teachers to finish what they want to say and reach a convenient point to break off. Ignoring remarks is less likely to work with younger pupils, who will frequently interpret the teacher's passivity as a signal that the question was not heard or unclear, and repeat it more loudly until they get a response.

Ignoring pupils' questions is unlikely to result in the interactive classroom environment that most teachers are searching for. It may, however, be appropriate if they have made it clear at the outset that interruptions are not permitted and the pupil has merely forgotten the rule. Inexperienced teachers, or those new to their classes, will have to persevere before pupils grasp that the comment has been ignored because they have not finished speaking.

To ask the pupil not to interrupt

If teachers ask a pupil not to interrupt on every occasion it occurs, they risk disrupting the smooth flow of their monologue and may affect the concentration of the whole class. On the other hand, regular calling out is disruptive in itself. Teachers have to balance the harm that comes from stopping and starting with that which comes from ignoring what is said. In the early stages of getting to know a class, it is preferable to spend time insisting on correct behaviour and not be too concerned with the loss of concentration. If teachers ask pupils not to interrupt and they respond with a protest or 'I only wanted to...' it is important not to be drawn into a dialogue or the query may as well have been answered in the first place and got it over with!

If several pupils interrupt at the same time, it is best to stop the lesson completely, remind everyone of the conventions,

and complete what you have to say as quickly as possible, before moving on to a settled task.

To accept the question or comment

Pupils' questions and comments can be extremely useful as a means of monitoring their understanding and the clarity of the teacher's explanation. If the conventions for interrupting are obeyed (such as raising a hand), and the question is taken, teachers can discover a lot about the way pupils' are thinking and reacting. If teachers want their pupils to become more questioning, they must either allow opportunities for questions to be placed at the time or encourage them to record their questions (by noting them on paper, for instance) for later consideration. It is not conducive to effective verbal communication if genuine questions are withheld and subsequently forgotten when the opportunity comes to ask them.

The problem for every teacher is knowing which strategy to use at any time when the passage of the lesson is interrupted by inappropriate behaviour. Imagine that you are calling a register and a pupil responds inappropriately. A number of possible responses are available to you (see the table below)

Table 18

Teacher responses to interruptions

- **Inert response**. *Continue regardless as if nothing had happened.*
- **Mute reaction**. *Continue without verbal comment but stare disapprovingly at the pupil.*
- **Reprimand**. *Stop, tell the pupil to be more sensible in future, then continue.*
- **Behaviourist comment**. *Stop, tell the pupil what you think of his behaviour, continue.*
- **Personal comment**. *Stop, tell the pupil what you think of him as an individual, continue.*
- **Disinterested comment**. *Stop, tell the pupil in a bored tone to act more sensibly, continue.*
- **Repetition**. *Repeat the pupil's name from the register as if he had not*

replied; wait for a sensible response; thank him coldly, continue.

- **Mockery**. *Stop, enquire with deliberate false concern about his welfare (speaking as he is with such a peculiar tone), tell him that you hope he will be better tomorrow, continue.*

- **Abrasive response**. *Stop, make an angry comment, including an instruction (such as to stand up for the remainder of the register).*

Activity 39

A boy answers a question in a falsetto voice and makes the other pupils giggle.

Consider your response using the examples in Table 18.

In making your decision for Activity 39, the following points should be borne in mind:

- A **disinterested comment** can take the fun out of the situation and make it seem pointless as it does not induce the reaction that was intended. On the other hand, such a verbal response may give the impression that you are unwilling to take firm action. It is more appropriate when you know the class well and your disinterest expresses the feelings of the majority.

- A **repetition** can be an extremely powerful verbal signal as it reinforces your authority and facilitates continuity. It may be necessary to repeat it several times (ignoring the pupil's protestations about having already answered) before receiving an acceptable reply. The repetition strategy is, however, unwise unless you are fairly certain that it will work.

If you use one of the other options, it is better to avoid any personal reference to the pupil concerned, either by a **direct comment** such as: 'As you don't seem to have the ability to answer in a sensible voice, I will have to teach you to do so at break time'. Or by a **public announcement** such as: 'I hope that no-one else is going to be as rude as Giles'. Neither of these comments is likely to assist the high quality communicative climate you are seeking for in your class.

The use of **personal remarks** is rarely worthwhile, even if they make you feel better for a short time; this type of public comment may raise a few cheap sniggers but quickly loses its impact and may induce resentment, even if the subject is deserving of a rebuke. Separating the pupil from the deed is the ideal aim.

- An **inert response** is sometimes the best one if other pupils' reactions to the silly behaviour is minimal. However, it is worth having a quiet word with the pupil at some time during the morning or following the lesson.

- It is not wise to use a **reprimand** unless it is out of character for the pupil concerned; in which case, a natural tone is sufficient to convey your displeasure.

- As a rule, it is far better to use a **behaviourist comment** about the pupil's action; for example, to tell the boy that you like to hear a normal tone, not a distorted one. Thus, to say: 'Giles. Speak in a normal tone please. Thank you'... and continue the register, is probably sufficient to make the point while maintaining the relationship.

- **Mockery** should rarely, if ever, be used, as sarcasm soon buries itself into a teacher's verbal responses and attitude, and becomes endemic. If you use mockery, select your pupil with great care and ensure that it is no more than gentle teasing at worst. Similarly, it is not worth making an **abrasive response** unless the offence has been committed before and earlier warnings have been ignored. Even under such conditions, use anger sparingly.

Whatever response you select, it is important to take account of the impression that your words and tone of voice are making upon all the pupils. If you get into the habit of speaking roughly or accusingly, your relationship with the whole class may be damaged irreparably. A friendly, calm and steady tone is preferable to a distant, accusatory one. On the rare occasion that you need to get angry, the contrast with your normally measured tone will create a far greater impact than if pupils are used to hearing you use impatient and intolerant comments.

- If the class is new to you or you are inexperienced, your lack of knowledge about the individual pupil's behaviour will probably mean that even if you select the best option (from the range above) there is a good chance that you will not select the most appropriate verbal comment to go with it. Many teachers choose to defuse the situation by using a mute reaction, a disinterested comment or a repetition.

■ If a mute comment is selected, it is worth considering a **delayed** response made at a later time when the immediacy of the incident has passed. Delayed responses have the advantage of allowing continuity of the process, giving you a few moments to decide upon appropriate action and choosing your own time (not the pupils') to make your point. On the other hand, an undue delay may be counter-productive if the rest of the class think that someone has got away with silly behaviour.

When small groups of pupils begin their own conversations

If two or three pupils begin a low level conversation while the teacher is addressing the whole class, it is important to show an awareness of what is going on with minimum disruption. Teachers may decide that is worth tolerating a quiet conversation for the sake of maintaining their rhythm of speech until they reach a natural break in the flow of words. In the meantime, teachers can use two strategies:

■ look towards the transgressors while still speaking and, if possible;

■ move physically closer to them.

At a convenient moment, it is useful to enquire whether the pupils have any questions about what has just been said. If they indicate that they do not, we have a choice about whether to press the issue by asking one of them to repeat something of what we have just said, or to tell them that we are not pleased when they are showing such behaviour. It is not worth allowing one of them to start a complaint about one of the other pupils in an attempt to sanitise their own actions. In such cases, we can merely repeat our hope that they will be polite enough to concentrate when we speak from now on, and we will offer them the same courtesy.

If you see pupils whispering together, it is not worth asking them what they were talking about as it may be something you do not want to hear about!

When insolent comments are made by disaffected pupils

Insolence cannot be tolerated. If teachers are struggling with class control, they may find that unacceptable comments surface from time to time. There are no simple solutions to restoring order in a disorderly class, but if teachers are trying to establish a responsive, interactive verbal environment and it is being hijacked by misbehaviour, it is important to go back to first principles about developing a satisfactory classroom environment. It is better to stop the flow of the lesson and confront the chief trouble maker than to struggle on and hope things will improve.

Teachers need to stay calm and confront the behaviour rather than the individual. Thus, to say 'Please do not call out during the lesson' in a firm tone is preferable to saying 'You are getting on my nerves, Margaret'. In the first case, the request is plain and unambiguous; further infractions invite sanctions. In the second case, the response is personally directed and acknowledges that pupil has succeeded in annoying you.

Pupil uncertainty about the boundaries of verbal interaction can have negative consequences for teachers. At worst it can result in teachers becoming angry, distracted and upset about the poor level of communication, and pupils becoming confused about the teacher's expectations and the lesson's purpose. If control issues become acute, the teacher is likely to reduce the amount of direct teaching and explanation in favour of written instructions and set texts (keeping their heads down). Sometimes, this has to act as an interim measure until the situation is more settled.

Activity 40

1. Allocate your pupils into three categories:
   - those pupils who normally conform;
   - those pupils who will get away with as much as they are allowed to;
   - those pupils who seem uncrushable.

It is likely that the first group is largest, then the second group, leaving a small number of individuals who are reluctant to play the game.

2. Encourage pupils in the second group to conform and contribute positively to lessons by adopting an upbeat and assertive approach yourself. Once you feel that the majority of this group are more responsive, turn your attention to the last group.

3. Aim eventually to involve everyone, but accept that it will take time and perseverance.

Large space activities

Large space activities provide opportunities and challenges for effective verbal communication, not only in ensuring that instructions are clearly stated and acted upon, but also for actively involving all pupils in group discussions about decisions and alternatives.

Because teachers are responsible for health and safety aspects of large space activities as well as the learning that takes place, it is essential that pupils are listening properly to instructions and grasp the importance of responding to verbal commands. Nowhere is this more important than during swimming lessons or handling large equipment. At critical moments, pupils need to be able to hear what teachers say and act upon commands. Similarly, if pupils are starting to indulge in horseplay and putting themselves or others at risk, the need for the teacher to speak in a strong, clear and authoritative tone is essential.

Pupil behaviour <u>inside</u> the classroom is governed by a number of constant factors, including the size of the room, availability of resources and regular procedures. When they are out of the classroom, however, pupils behaviour, verbal interaction and volume, can alter considerably. The quiet, unassuming fellow, sitting placidly doing his maths, can be transformed into a loud, hectoring type on the games field. The friendly, helpful young lady in conversational English may become arrogant and fierce when with a group of friends in the playground. Even a change of room can make a difference; the confident, cocky girl in her own room is sometimes passive and insecure in a different environment. The annoying boy who seems to delight in calling out during lessons becomes subdued in a public performance of a piece of drama. Such is life.

In open space activities such as drama, pupils should be offered the chance to speculate and engage with alternatives. They have the right to expect that teachers will listen carefully to their ideas and respond positively and constructively.

Teachers need to change their own behaviour in different circumstances and moderate their speech in a manner appropriate to the situation. Large space activities demand slower and more carefully articulated speech. Giving instructions to pupils in advance of a school production requires a specificity and assertiveness that is often unnecessary in the confines of the classroom. Careful organisation and management, together with well-judged voice production, will help to ensure that control problems are minimised in out-of-classroom contexts.

Similarly, <u>motivation factors</u> will be different, depending upon the specific circumstances: the boy who moans and groans about a writing task may need little encouragement to play basketball; the girl who insists that she is hopeless at maths may spring to life in a dance session. Some pupils are inclined to want to 'take over' during large space lessons, so teachers need to be on top of the job if they are to control events, while at the same time ensuring that pupils have opportunity to verbally contribute ideas and offer creative solutions to issues as much as they would in the classroom setting.

Case studies

Case 1: The anti-social pupil

Nine year-old Colin is beginning to test your patience. He won't sit still in his chair and walks around disturbing other pupils. Angela complains that he has poked her with a pencil. Colin retorts that she had refused to lend him a sharpener. He is sullen and reluctant to settle down to work. Other teachers have told you about his anti-social behaviour and the disturbed family situation.

- What verbal skills do you need to deal with Colin?
- What verbal strategies might be employed to improve the situation?

Case 2: The disaffected pupil

Six year old Lillie does not seem willing to try hard with her work. She stares at the page but won't actively do anything unless prompted. She sometimes gets part way through some work and gives up. Several times she has deliberately crumpled up her work or scribbled on it. Most recently you found several pupils' work defaced. Lillie denies that she is responsible but you are almost certain that she is.

- What lies at the heart of the problem?
- How will you go about motivating Lillie?
- What other strategies are available to rectify the situation in the short term?

Case 3: The isolated pupil

Twelve year old Kareena has a bright, engaging personality and is usually the first to volunteer for jobs. She relates easily to adults but is not popular with her peers. She is academically slow and uses every excuse to avoid work. When challenged she pleads helplessness and, following your patient explanation, assures you that she understands and works for a short time. However, things soon return to the familiar pattern.

- How significant is Kareena's isolation from her peers?
- What positive aspects can be built upon?
- What strategies can you employ to deal with her 'learned helplessness'?

Case 4: The unmotivated pupil

Fifteen year-old Craig plays only a minor part in collaborative activities. He simply sits around, lolling about and yawning. The others in the group have given up trying to involve him, so he is becoming increasingly detached from the work. When you encourage him to get more involved, he apologises, concentrates for a few minutes, then regresses to his usual state. One of the pupils confidentially asks you if they can have someone different in the group.

■ Is there anyway to enthuse Craig?
■ How much is his learning being damaged by his poor communications skills?
■ What difference might inclusion in a different group make?

Chapter 7

Speaking to adults

Speaking in public is just like acting, even if you are acting the part of yourself.

(Hambly, 1987)

Despite the advent of information and communication technology, the art of public speaking remains an essential skill for all teachers, especially those with responsibilities as a curriculum leader, head of department, governor or senior manager. The ability to put across a message succinctly and accurately is a requirement for anyone who aspires to influence others.

Engaging hearts and minds

Adults respond to speakers who not only engage their minds by providing relevant and interesting information, ideas and strategies, but also touch their hearts, by convincing them that the speaker is aware of the listeners' emotional needs, aspirations, hopes, fears and dilemmas. If the audience feels that the speaker is unaware of the realities facing them, even the greatest talk will not be well received. If the audience feels that the speaker understands their situation, they will adopt a more sympathetic and supportive attitude.

Activity 41

1. Write down the names of two education speakers who have impressed you and the things that characterised their talks, selecting from the following:

- good, clear tone;
- engaging personality;
- grasp of the subject matter;
- well presented material;
- well structured talk;
- appropriate level of information;
- well paced;
- relevant and interesting;
- able to empathise with the listeners.

2. List the attributes under three headings: a) those you possess strongly; b) those in which you are adequately strong and c) those that are less strong.

3. Using the information from this book, set out an action plan to move those areas that are less strong into the 'adequately strong' column.

Table 19

Matching the speech form and purpose

- *If the main purpose is to justify a course of action,* **explanation** *is most relevant.*
- *If it is to relay something, then* **description** *is likely to form the majority of the talk.*
- *If it is to take the audience into new realms of understanding, then* **exposition** *is important.*
- *If it is to show a practical skill or technique, the ability to* **demonstrate** *clearly and effectively while describing and explaining, becomes a priority.*

Once the main purpose of the talk is clear, you can make a decision about the dominant style you will use and the resources that are needed to support it.

The impact of your words

Although it is not possible to predict with accuracy what listeners will recall, it is important for speakers to be clear about what they hope people will remember. As such, they need to establish beforehand the main purpose of the talk and the key things they want to emphasise. In doing so, there are two questions to consider:

- What are the listeners expecting to hear?
- What are the points that speakers want them to know that they did not know, or were not sure of, before they began?

If we relate these questions to three commonly experienced situations, namely: colleagues at a staff meeting; parents' meeting; interviews, we can begin to map out a plan of action for each circumstance.

What my listeners are expecting to hear

With colleagues: You should have contacted them before the meeting and given them a broad outline of your intentions and any important details to browse through. A short briefing paper (keep the detail to a minimum) can save you a lot of time introducing the topic, answering questions about the purpose of the session and settling colleagues to the task at the start of the meeting.

With parents: Parents attending an open evening should have received some information about the purpose of the meeting and why it is important that they attend. If they turn up expecting to hear something different, attitudes may harden.

With an interview panel: An interview panel will have drawn up a list of things they want to ascertain from you during the interview. As part of your preparation, write down four or five key points that you would want to hear, were you a member of the panel interviewing yourself.

What I want them to know

With colleagues: Introduce your talk to colleagues by telling them something of the background to the issue on the agenda, re-stating the specific intentions of the meeting, and clarifying what you hope to achieve in the time available. In your preparation, make sure that you have a good grasp of these elements so that you can begin confidently and give the impression that you know what you are doing. Introduce your points deliberately. Do not rush things through, but beware of allowing too much free conversation or you may lose your hold on the proceedings. Tired teachers have been known to dissolve into fits of giggles, which completely wreck the meeting.

With parents: Depending upon the purpose of the parents' meeting, you will need to be quite certain about what you want them to know or understand. Remember that your credibility as a professional is being scrutinised as you address your audience. After thanking them for coming, remind the parents precisely why they have come and why it is important. You may be surprised how many busy parents turn up for school events unclear about the purpose until you tell them! By the end of the talk you should recapitulate and ensure that you conclude positively.

With an interview panel: Although the panel will have its own agenda, you have to ensure that as well as answering their questions directly, you take every opportunity to slip in some snippets of information which will enhance the impression you create. Many members are happy to pick up something of interest that you have said and use it as part of the next question, so it is worth placing your 'additional' point near to the end of what you are saying so that it can be used by the next questioner.

The special occasion

If you are invited to speak at a special occasion, you need to start your preparations well in advance to make the best of your opportunity. More experienced speakers learn to cope with the unexpected and fashion their talk according to the circumstances they meet on arrival, but for the majority of people, careful and thorough advance preparation is essential. The stages of preparation can be summarised under three broad headings:

- accepting the invitation and clarifying the details;
- designing a plan of action;
- on the day.

If you receive an invitation to speak, make sure that you have spoken to the co-ordinator and clarified in detail the nature of the engagement in terms of the following.

The exact time it will occur, including an approximate finishing time

Find out if there are any logistical factors which may influence the arrangements, such as the location of the car park, the number of stairs to climb (especially if you have to carry equipment), and how far in advance of the start time the room is available.

What is expected of you

Clarify what your talk is meant to be about and the likely constituency of the listeners: Are they knowledgeable or coming to the ideas for the first time? Will they want to ask questions or sit quietly and listen? Have they been to similar meetings before? Is your talk one of a series? If so, where does what you say fit in the overall plan?

The physical context

The physical context will make a difference to the way in which you structure your talk. For instance, physical factors such as the size of the room, whether it is carpeted, whether lighting is adequate to read your notes, and whether you are situated on a stage or on the level, are relevant to the way you prepare your delivery.

Designing a plan of action

Organise what you want to say into three or four main categories

The number of categories will vary according to the subject, but it is difficult for listeners to keep track of more than four points. Preachers traditionally use just three main points in a sermon in the belief that a larger number will result in the congregation losing interest or concentration. The broad categories will include:

- Introductory remarks, including scene setting.
- The main points.
- Concluding remarks, including task setting (where appropriate).

The night before

Read through your notes for the last time, concentrating on the vital opening sentences. Go through the items very carefully, picturing in your mind's eye where you will need each piece of equipment or visual aid. It is surprisingly easy to forget obvious and essential resources (such as your notes!), so leave nothing to chance.

On the day

There are a number of factors which affect the quality of your voice, including the atmosphere in which you live and work, and the use you make of your voice throughout the day. Excessive use of your voice before the meeting will spoil your ability to speak clearly in public, so avoid shouting or straining your vocal chords through (say) too much singing or shouting. Use some of the exercises from Chapter 2 to relax your throat muscles and get your breathing under control.

In the pressure of the moment it is easy to forget the most fundamental principles for good speech, so remember to:

- open your mouth and bring words to the front of your mouth;
- use your lips and move your mouth freely (practise this by saying words in sentences slowly and exaggerating the mouth movement);

■ relax your throat muscles and stand upright;

■ ease into your speaking but pay attention to consonants and careful articulation;

■ emphasise key words and phrases;

■ make good use of pauses: they allow you to breath easily for a moment, gives the audience an opportunity to gather their thoughts and, in some cases, gives you time to think of your next point.

Rehearsing

Hambly (1987) suggests that it is a good idea to rehearse your talk in front of a mirror and record it on cassette. Standing in front of a mirror allows you to check whether you have a correct posture, the number of times you need to look at your notes and if you are making any strange facial expressions. Recording your talk on cassette will help you determine whether it makes sense, whether you are speaking clearly and delivering at an appropriate pace, and whether there are points at which you lose the thread of what you are saying and need to give it more thought.

If you are including support material (such as visual aids) into the presentation, make sure that you rehearse them as thoroughly as the speech itself.

Finally, remember to **time** the whole presentation.

Never write too much on a single overhead transparency. Only use key words and phrases. If the audience need a lot of information, put the detail on a handout, made available after the talk.

Always leave up the transparency a little longer than you think is necessary.

Read it or remember it?

A decision about whether to read from a prepared text or use summary notes and rely upon your memory and experience to develop points as they arise, depends upon three factors:

Your familiarity with the material

If you have given the talk before, you may not need the full text in front of you. If you are giving the talk for the first time, you may feel safer with the whole speech in written form.

The need to establish eye contact with the audience

If you consider that eye contact is particularly important (for instance, giving a talk to anxious parents), it is worth reducing the extent to which you have to rely on notes. If eye contact is less important (for instance, giving a speech to a leavers' day audience), reading from full notes is more acceptable.

The delicacy of the subject

If you are talking about a subject such as child abuse or bullying, you obviously need to choose your words with great care, in which case reading from a prepared script may be wise.

Activity 42

1. Without using notes, summarise your talk in two minutes.

2. With the aid of some brief notes, summarise your talk in under five minutes.

3. On the basis of 1 and 2 decide whether you need access to full 'verbatim' notes.

Structuring the talk

Beginning

Never hurry the first part of your talk. Breath deeply, stretch your spine by standing upright, take your time and look carefully around the room, establishing eye contact with as many persons as possible. A gentle smile is often helpful, as it carries a non-threatening message and helps to invoke your listeners' curiosity.

When others are putting you under pressure to speak, they will simply have to wait until you are ready! Rushing can be your ruin. Count to three.

Once the formalities are over, **clarify with the listeners what is happening**. For instance, if you are going to speak for twenty minutes before moving into a question-and-answer session, say so. If you are going to invite participation throughout, say so. Don't make the mistake of inviting the listeners to interject with questions or comments if, in reality, you want to have a clear run.

Activity 43

1. Rehearse the first minute of your talk in front of a trusted friend.
2. Ask the friend to give you feedback based on:
   - your general posture;
   - the clarity of your opening remarks;
   - the sense of anticipation you evoke in your listener;
   - the tone and speed of your delivery;
   - your ability to explain what the talk is about.

Involving the audience

Make a positive start. Tell a short story; ask for a 'hands-up' to a question; show a relevant object; pose a dilemma; tell a genuinely amusing story about something you recently encountered. (Not, however, a joke, unless you are good at telling them.)

Activity 44

1. Rehearse ways of engaging your audience through:

- telling a short story;
- asking a question and anticipating possible responses;
- referring to a visual aid;
- posing a dilemma;
- telling a short, amusing story.

2. Deliberate on which of the methods above facilitates a positive start to your talk.

Developing the talk

The importance of being clear about your main ideas cannot be over-stated. They act as 'coat hangers' around which to hang your subsidiary points. Every main point will have several supporting points which can be separately developed, but the audience must be able to see the relationship between them.

Analogies should be obvious ones; an audience should not have to think too deeply about the meaning or they will still be thinking about it when you have moved on to your next point. Keep them sharp and accessible to the listeners.

Illustrative stories are best used as specific examples after making a general point. They provide a useful interlude in the body of the talk and allow listeners to relax for a few moments. True stories are generally preferable to contrived ones.

The final phase

The final phase of the talk should be concise but unhurried. Don't say 'finally' unless you really mean it. Review the main points of the talk. Don't start saying something new.

If possible, give the listeners something to take away with them: a thought; a proposition; an idea; something to discover, try or investigate. If a question-and-answer time is to follow, raise a few key questions yourself and areas of uncertainty arising from what you have said as a spur for questions.

Activity 45

1. Record alternative conclusions to your talk on tape.

2. Decide which one sounds the most convincing and natural by sitting and listening as though you were a member of the audience, based on the following criteria:

- its conciseness;
- the way it complements the earlier part of the talk;
- the extent to which it is a genuine conclusion rather than an extension to the main talk;
- the feeling of satisfaction and 'completeness' it leaves.

Things to avoid saying

Some speakers do not help themselves by making comments which give the impression that they are not in charge of their material or confident enough to handle a public occasion. The table below contains some examples of unwise statements that may act against your best interests.

Table 19

Unwise statements

- **'You're probably wondering where all this is getting us'**... *don't put negative ideas in their minds!*

- **'I will return to this later on'**... *unless the audience are expecting a long haul. Better to say 'I will return to this in a moment' which gives the audience hope that the talk won't be too lengthy!*

- **'I expect you want me to shut up and let you get a word in edgeways'**... *as anything you say from that point onward will be perceived as a hindrance to letting them contribute. Better to say: 'I want to spend five more minutes concluding this part of the talk, then I will take a few questions before we see the video extract'.*

- **'You've been a wonderful audience'** *or any other shallow remarks. If you are genuinely thankful for their close attention, say so sincerely and sit down.*

When it is all over

Every form of public speaking requires a lot of effort and uses a considerable amount of energy. Give yourself some space after the meeting to relax and recover. Accept praise modestly; accept the lack of it with dignity.

One thing is certain, with perseverance and practice, you will gradually gain confidence in speaking and become a more assured and effective verbal communicator.

References

Barnes, D. (1975) *From Communication to Curriculum*. Harmondsworth: Penguin Books.

Bird, J. (1990) 'Developing real life learning' in Craig, I. (ed.) *Managing the Primary Classroom*. Harlow: Longman.

Bolton, R. (1979) *People Skills*. New York: Simon & Schuster.

Bostock, L. (1994) *Speaking in Public: A Guide to Speaking with Confidence*. Glasgow: Harper Collins.

Bowers, C.A. and Flinders, D.J. (1990) *Responsive Teaching*. New York: Teachers College Press.

Brown, G.A. and Atkins, M. (1987) *Effective Teaching in Higher Education*. London: Methuen.

Brown, G.A. and Wragg, E.C. (1993) *Questioning*. London: Routledge.

Bruner, J. (1966) *Toward a Theory of Instruction*. Cambridge, Mass.: Belknap Press.

Bryson, J. (1998) *Effective Teaching Skills: Effective Classroom Management*. London: Hodder and Stoughton.

Cullingford, C. (1995) *The Effective Teacher*. London: Cassell.

Currie, M. and Bromfield, C. (1998) *Circle Time In-Service Training Manual*. Tamworth: NASEN.

Dean, J. (1992) *Organising Learning in the Primary School Classroom*. London: Routledge.

Delamont, S. (1976) *Interaction in the Classroom*. London: Methuen.

Department for Education/Welsh Office (1995) *English in the National Curriculum*. London: HMSO.

Department for Education and Employment (1997) *The Implementation of the National Literacy Strategy*. DfEE: London.

Dougill, P. and Knott, R. (1988) *The Primary Language Book*. Milton Keynes: Open University Press.

Edwards, A.D. and Furlong, V.J. (1978) *The Language of Teaching*.

London: Heinemann Educational.

Edwards, A.D. and Westgate, D.P.G. (1994) *Investigating Classroom Talk* (2nd edition). London: Falmer Press.

Fisher, R. (1990) *Teaching Children to Think.* Cheltenham: Stanley Thornes.

Fisher, R. (1995) *Teaching Children to Learn.* Cheltenham: Stanley Thornes Publishers.

Flanders, N. (1970) *Analysing Teaching Behaviour.* Reading, Mass.: Addison-Wesley.

Fontana, D. (1994, 2nd edition) *Classroom Control.* Leicester: BPS Books.

Fox, R. (1995) 'Development and learning' in Desforges, C. (ed.) *An Introduction to Teaching.* Oxford; Blackwell.

Good, T. and Brophy, J. (1986) 'Teacher behaviour and student achievement' in Wuttrock, M. (ed) *Handbook of Research On Teaching.* New York: Macmillan.

Hambly, K. (1987) *How to Improve Your Confidence.* London: Sheldon.

Hayes, D. (1997) *Success on Your Teaching Experience.* London: Hodder and Stoughton.

Hitchman, P.J. (1977) *The Voice and Speech of Teachers.* Nottingham: Nottingham University School of Education.

Horner, A.M. (1970) *Movement, Voice and Speech.* London: Methuen.

Howard, G. (1980) *Getting Through: Making Words Work For You.* London: David & Charles.

Hulbert, H.H. (1932) *Voice Training in Speech and Song.* London: University Tutorial Press.

Hymes, D. (1972) 'On communicative competence' in Pride, J. and Holmes, J. (eds), *Sociolinguistics.* Harmondsworth: Penguin Books.

Jones, A. and Buttrey, J. (1970) *Children and Stories.* Oxford: Basil Blackwell.

Kerry, T. (1998) *Effective Teaching Skills: Questioning and Explaining in Classrooms.* London: Hodder and Stoughton.

Laslett, R. and Smith, C. (1984) *Effective Classroom Management.*

London: Croom Helm.

Linklater, K. (1976) *Freeing the Natural Voice.* New York: Drama Book Specialists.

Nelson-Jones, R. (1986) *Human Relationship Skills.* London: Cassell.

Nuthall, G.A. and Lawrence, P.J. (1965) *Thinking in the Classroom.* Wellington, N.Z.: New Zealand Council for Educational Research.

Pollard, A. (1997) *Reflective Teaching in the Primary School* (3rd edition). London: Cassell.

Proctor, A., Entwistle, M., Judge, B., and McKenzie-Murdoch, S. (1995) *Learning to Teach in the Primary Classroom.* London: Routledge.

Pye, J. (1987) *Invisible Children.* Oxford: Oxford University Press.

Qualifications and Curriculum Authority (1997) *Monitoring the School Curriculum: Reporting to Schools.* London: QCA Publications.

Rodenburg, P. (1992) *The Right To Speak: Working With The Voice.* London: Methuen Drama.

Sansom, C. (1978) *Speech and Communication in the Primary School.* London: Black.

Silverstein, A. (ed, 1974) *Human Communication: Theoretical Explorations.* New Jersey: Lawrence Erlbaum Associates.

Smith, R. (1993) *Managing Pupil Behaviour in School and Classroom.* Lancaster: Framework Press.

Tizzard, B. and Hughes, M. (1984) *Young Children Learning: Talking and Thinking at Home and at School.* London: Fontana.

Tough, J. (1985) *Talking and Learning.* London: Ward Lock Educational/Schools Council.

Whitaker, P. (1997) *Primary Schools and the Future.* Buckingham: Open University Press.

Woods, P. (1987) 'Managing the primary teacher's role' in Delamont, S. (ed) *The Primary Teacher.* London: Falmer Press.

Wragg, E.C. (ed. 1984) *Classroom Teaching Skills.* London: Croom Helm.

Wragg, E.C. and Brown, G.A. (1993) *Explaining.* London: Routledge.

Index

Articulation 22–3, 30–1, 33–4, 39–40

Audience xii, 30, 55–7, 138–9, 145, 147–8

Authoritarian teachers 117–8

Behaviourist theory 86–88

Behaviours
  aggressive 120–2
  assertive 120–2
  authoritarian 117–9
  decisive 117, 119
  submissive 120

Body language 63–4

Classroom climate 47–8, 71–2, 77–82, 90–3

Classroom layout 110–12

Collaborating 100–101, 103–5

Communicating
  effectiveness 44–6, 56–7, 75–6
  quality 78–82, 116–7
  networks 97–103
  with audience 1–2, 55–8, 108–9, 145–8

Confidence 35–40, 85–6, 92–3

Constructivist theory 88–9

Describing 13–14, 16–17, 104, 139

Discipline
  conventions 123–5

disorder 76, 78, 132–3
  humour 125
  insolence 133
  interruptions 127–130
  problems 126–7
  responding to comments 129–132

Explaining 14–15, 17, 60–2

Group work
  constraints 48–9, 132
  organization 49–51, 92–3, 100–103

Inflection 32

Large space activities 124, 134–5

Learning environment 90–3, 99–100

Learning theories 86–90

Lessons
  preparation 37, 111
  stages 52–3, 126

Listening skills 48, 53–4

Literacy hour 108

Mistakes 92, 105–6

Motivation 114–7, 125, 135–7

Narrative 12–13

National Curriculum 44–6

Pitch 31–2, 38–9
Preparation
    for speaking 18–19, 37, 143–4
    rehearsing 69–72, 94

Questions 104–7

Reading aloud 112
Rehearsing 144
Relationships 71–2, 74, 77–9,
    115–6, 130–2

Social constructivist theory 89–90
Speaking
    and listening xiv–xv, 44–66, 140–1
    articulation 33–4
    clarity 18–43
    delivery 30–5, 39–40
    effectiveness 62–3, 80
    emphasis 32–3
    function 10–11
    implicit and explicit 123–4
    intonation 112
    pitch 31–2, 38–9
    rhythm 34–5
    speed 9–10, 29–30
Special occasion 142

Talking
    and learning 67–8, 72–4, 84–6,
    90–7

contexts 7, 11, 72–4, 142
conventions 8–9, 83
initiating 68, 104–7
structure 12–17, 146–8
to adults 138–149
Teacher types 117–23
Teaching
    lesson structure 73–4, 85–6,
    93–6, 108–9, 126
    listening to pupils 53–5, 80–2
    pupil involvement 44–8, 68–9,
    76–7, 82–3, 99–101, 106–8
    teacher's role 51–3, 75–7,
    98–100, 103–9
Tone 26, 112–3

Understanding 42–3, 68–74,
    94–5,

Verbal climate 77–82, 90–3,
    108–9, 115–7
Verbal strategies 117–9, 122–3
Vocabulary 40–2, 46, 68–71
Voice
    breathing 19, 23–4, 27–8
    care of 18–19, 21–30, 38–40
    quality 20, 38–40, 62
    volume 25–6, 39

Whole class teaching 49–51, 102
Word pictures 58–9
Word power 2–5, 64–6, 115–7,
    140–1